LIFELINE

LIFELINE

A BRITISH CASUALTY CLEARING STATION ON THE WESTERN FRONT, 1918

IAIN GORDON

FOREWORD BY MAJOR GENERAL M. J. VON BERTELE
DIRECTOR-GENERAL ARMY MEDICAL SERVICES

In memory of the 7,073 members of the Army Medical Services killed in action during the First World War.

By the same author:
Soldier of the Raj
Admiral of the Blue
Bloodline

First published 2013

The History Press
The Mill, Brimscombe Port
Stroud, Gloucestershire, GL5 2QG
www.thehistorypress.co.uk

British Library Cataloguing in Publication Data.
A catalogue record for this book is available from the British Library.

isbn 978 0 7524 8996 4

Typesetting and origination by The History Press
Printed in Great Britain

CONTENTS

LIST OF PLATES

Permission to reproduce illustrations used in this book is gratefully acknowledged as follows:

Between pages 32/33:

001 A Casualty Clearing Station on the Western Front. Daryl Lindsay © Wellcome Library, London

002 Collecting the wounded from a battlefield. Daryl Lindsay © Wellcome Library, London

003 Aerial photograph of the hospital sites at Grévillers, one on either side of the road. Note the red crosses for aerial recognition and the cemetery (lower left). © Imperial War Museum (Box 871 1918)

004 The same positions on a contemporary trench map. The castellated lines represent German trenches and the Xs are barbed wire entanglements. © National Archives

005 The hospital sites at Grévillers today with Grévillers village and church in the background (left) and the CWGC cemetery (right). The hospital railway siding would have run roughly along the dividing line of the short and long grass in the field on the left.

006 29 Casualty Clearing Station at Grévillers on 21 March 1918, the first day of the big German offensive. The wards in 29CCS and 3CCS are overflowing and the ambulance trains cannot arrive quickly enough to deal with the massive intake of casualties. Here, patients on stretchers lie in rows beside the railway siding waiting for the next train to evacuate them to a base hospital. By noon the following day, the two hospitals will have admitted more than 4,000 wounded men. © Army Medical Services Museum

007 Grévillers British War Cemetery in the early 1920s with the wooden crosses still in place. © Commonwealth War Graves Commission

008 The cemetery today.

009 No. 33 Ambulance Train stands on the hospital siding at Grévillers on 27 November 1917. The following day it left for base hospital with 99 patients from 29CCS. The main Achiet-Marcoing railway line is in the foreground. © Imperial War museum (Q47147)

010 The same view today. The main line is now derelict and the hospital siding has been removed. Inset: The derelict main line.

011 An Advanced Dressing Station close behind the frontline. © Wellcome Library, London

012 A Regimental Aid Post in the trenches. © Wellcome Library, London

013 'Nightfall' – A poignant picture of blinded and partially blinded men, each with a hand on the shoulder of the man in front for guidance, in a shuffling queue for treatment at a Casualty Clearing Station. © Wellcome Library, London

014 German prisoners assist British stretcher bearers to gather the wounded on a battlefield for transportation to a Field Ambulance or Casualty Clearing Station. © Wellcome Library, London

027 Lieutenant Colonel James Allman Armstrong IMS Civil Surgeon Cawnpore. (Father-in-Law of JCGC)

028 Colonel James Charles Gordon Carmichael IMS Civil Surgeon Fort William, Calcutta. (Father of JCGC)

029 Hilda Sade Carmichael (née Armstrong). (Wife of JCGC)

030 Colonel Donald Roy Gordon Carmichael. (Son of JCGC)

031 James Charles Gordon Carmichael on commissioning as a Lieutenant RAMC in 1902.

032 A kilted Highland soldier outside the Collecting Post for Walking Cases at 69 Field Ambulance amidst the desolation of the Western Front. © Wellcome Library, London

033 A Dental Officer attached to a Casualty Clearing Station. There was an acute shortage of dentists at the beginning of the war until the C-in-C instituted a recruiting drive following severe toothache for which he had difficulty in obtaining treatment. © Wellcome Library, London

Between pages 96/97:

034 The 'Hospital Valley' at Gézaincourt in which two, and sometimes three, Casualty Clearing Stations were located. The area resembled 'a vast tented city'.

035 The disused railway halt at Gézaincourt from where a continuous succession of Ambulance Trains evacuated wounded to base hospitals, having received treatment and emergency surgery at the CCSs in the valley. The Cross of Sacrifice in Bagneux CWGC Cemetery can be seen on the left.

036 The grave of Private R.G. Crompton, West Yorkshire Regiment, who was buried in the Bagneux Cemetery, Gézaincourt on 25 April 1918.

He was aged 19. The official photograph taken in the early 1920s, showing the original wooden cross, and sent to the family when they requested details. © Commonwealth War Graves Commission

037 The same grave today. © Richard Crompton

038 A photograph of Private J.W. Laurenson, Durham Light Infantry, who died of wounds in 29CCS on 27 August 1918. The photograph was left recently with the Cemetery Visitors' Book by a relative visiting the site.

039 A view of the Bagneux CWGC Cemetery at Gézaincourt with the 'Hospital Valley' beyond.

040 Graves of two Coolies of the Chinese Labour Corps.

041 Graves of the Canadian Medical personnel killed in the German raid on the hospital at Doullens.

042 RAMC ambulances collect the wounded from a battlefield.

043 Soldiers struggle to free an ambulance stuck in the mud.

044 The Padre writes a letter home for a wounded soldier.

045 Personnel of 29th Casualty Clearing Station, Germany 1919. The CO in an overcoat sits between the Chaplain and the Quartermaster.

046 The French hospice at Warloy-Baillon where the officers of 29CCS slept on the floor of the porter's lodge during their retreat from Grévillers on 25 March 1918.

047 29th Casualty Clearing Station Bonn, 1919. A ward in the converted chapel. © Imperial War Museum (Q3747)

048 The 19th century St. Marien's Hospital in Bonn in which 29CCS was located. © Imperial War Museum (Q3746)

ABBREVIATIONS

AAMC	Australian Army Medical Corps
AB	Able Seaman
ADMS	Assistant Director of Medical Services
ADS	Advanced Dressing Station
AG	Adjutant General
AMS	Army Medical Services
ANS	Army Nursing Services
ANZAC	Australian and New Zealand Army Corps
Arty	Artillery
ASC	Army Service Corps
Asst	Assistant
AT	Ambulance Train
BEF	British Expeditionary Force
BRCS	British Red Cross Society
Brig. Gen.	Brigadier General
Bn	Battalion
CAMC	Canadian Army Medical Corps
Capt.	Captain
CCS	Casualty Clearing Station
CIGS	Chief of Imperial General Staff
C-in-C	Commander-in-Chief
CO	Commanding Officer
Col	Colonel
CP	Collecting Post

Cpl	Corporal
CWGC	Commonwealth War Graves Commission
DAG	Deputy Adjutant General
DCM	Distinguished Conduct Medal
DDMS	Deputy Director of Medical Services
DMS	Director of Medical Services
DGAMS	Director General of Army Medical Services
Div.	Division
DLI	Durham Light Infantry
DSO	Distinguished Service Order
Dvr	Driver
FA	Field Ambulance
FM	Field Marshal
Gen.	General
GH	General Hospital
GHQ	General Headquarters
GOC	General Officer Commanding
Gnr	Gunner
HQ	Headquarters
Inf.	Infantry
IMS	Indian Medical Service
KSLI	King's Shropshire Light Infantry
Lt	Lieutenant
Lt Gen.	Lieutenant General
Lt Col	Lieutenant Colonel
L/Cpl	Lance Corporal
L/Sea.	Leading Seaman
MAC	Motor Ambulance Convoy
Maj.	Major
Maj. Gen.	Major General
MC	Military Cross
MDS	Main Dressing Station
MGC	Machine Gun Corps
MO	Medical Officer
MORC	Medical Officer Reserve Corps (US Army)
MSM	Military Service Medal
NCO	Non-Commissioned Officer

N FUS	Northumberland Fusiliers
NYD(N)	Not Yet Diagnosed (Neurological / Nervous)
NZMC	New Zealand Medical Corps
OBE	Order of the British Empire
OC	Officer Commanding
PMO	Principal Medical Officer
Pnr	Pioneer
PO	Petty Officer
POW	Prisoner of War
Pte	Private
QAIMNS	Queen Alexandra's Imperial Military Nursing Service
QM	Quartermaster
QMAAC	Queen Mary's Auxiliary Army Corps
QMG	Quartermaster General
QMS	Quartermaster Sergeant
RAChD	Royal Army Chaplains Department
RAF	Royal Air Force
RAMC	Royal Army Medical Corps
RAP	Regimental Aid Post
RE	Royal Engineers
Regt	Regiment
Revd	Reverend
RFA	Royal Field Artillery
RFC	Royal Flying Corps
RGA	Royal Garrison Artillery
RHA	Royal Horse Artillery
RMO	Regimental Medical Officer
RN	Royal Navy
RP	Relay Post
RSM	Regimental Sergeant Major
RTO	Rail Transport Officer
RWF	Royal Welsh Fusiliers
Sgt	Sergeant
SH	Stationary Hospital
SIW	Self-Inflicted Wound
SMO	Senior Medical Officer
Sub-Lt	Sub Lieutenant

Surg.	Surgeon / Surgical
TAT	Temporary Ambulance Train
TC	Temporary Commission
TF	Territorial Force
TFNS	Territorial Force Nursing Service
VAD	Voluntary Aid Detachment
VC	Victoria Cross
VD	Venereal Disease
WO	War Office, Warrant Officer
WWCS	Walking Wounded Collection Station

FOREWORD

BY MAJOR GENERAL M. J. VON BERTELE, QHS, OBE
DIRECTOR GENERAL ARMY MEDICAL SERVICES

Anyone who has served on operations with the medical services over the last ten years will read this account of a casualty clearing station in the last months of the First World War with a mixture of awe and familiarity. All of the lessons are writ large, and most seem to have been learned at that time, but that casualty care should be managed on such a scale and at such pace leaves the reader open-mouthed. Essentially, this is a detailed account of CCS 29 (there were 74 in total and over 200 field ambulances), researched and described in intimate detail, in the final push in 1918. They were driven first one way as the Germans attacked, and then the other as the Allies, eventually joined by America, drove them out of France. At every turn the much later observation of Rupert Smith was proved true: 'The only certain result of your plan will be casualties, mainly the enemy if it is a good plan, yours if it is not,' and what numbers; it was not uncommon for a CCS to admit more than 1,000 casualties in a day, and to operate, treat and evacuate them all.

The DMS planners seemed up to the task; the speed of planning, of movement, anticipation, operational tempo, and opening and closing of medical units, was a prominent feature of the campaign. The preferred means of movement seems to have been rail, both for logistical moves and the evacuation of casualties. A CCS filled twenty railway wagons, and the ambulance trains could carry 700 casualties. It demonstrated the utility and flexibility of ground evacuation in an era before aviation. When rail and truck failed, the men were forced to redeploy on foot and were married up with the next trainload of medical stores that became available. It is hard to comprehend the scale of the organisational challenge in such seemingly chaotic circumstances, but in the fourth year of the war it ran with industrial precision and the commanding officer, Lieutenant Colonel Carmichael, even found time to write to his wife in Malta, using a postal service that was quicker than that enjoyed today. Throughout, we are reminded that the sick and diseased, notably those unfortunate souls who had taken comfort from local prostitutes, formed a core of inpatients, and the VD patients even provided a useful source of unskilled labour, not afforded the luxury of rearwards evacuation.

This is an account that is immediately recognisable by the common features that persist to this day. Efficient clearance of casualties from the battlefield, their effective triage, treatment and onward evacuation, is as essential to the maintenance of the moral component now, as it was then, if armies and their commanders are to retain the ability to prosecute wars.

Major General M. J. von Bertele, QHS, OBE
Director General Army Medical Services

ACKNOWLEDGEMENTS

As with any writer whose work depends upon extensive research, I am again made conscious of the debt of gratitude which we owe to all those dedicated people who work in the country's libraries, museums and archives to preserve the documents which form our national heritage and to which they direct us with good nature and expertise when we seek to consult them.

I thank them all, and would particularly mention Simon Wilson of The Wellcome Trust, Vanessa Rodnight of the National Army Museum, Freddie Hollom of the Imperial War Museum, Captain Peter Starling and his staff at the Army Medical Services Museum and Ian Small of the Commonwealth War Graves Commission.

I am also, as usual, deeply grateful to my friends Natalie Gilbert, Ronald Dunning and John Brain for their help with research, and, as ever, to my wife Anthea for her meticulous and professional copy-editing.

Last, but not least, I must thank the present Director General Army Medical Services, Major General Michael von Bertele, for sparing the time in his very busy life to read the drafts and contribute the foreword.

Iain Gordon
Barnstaple, Devon

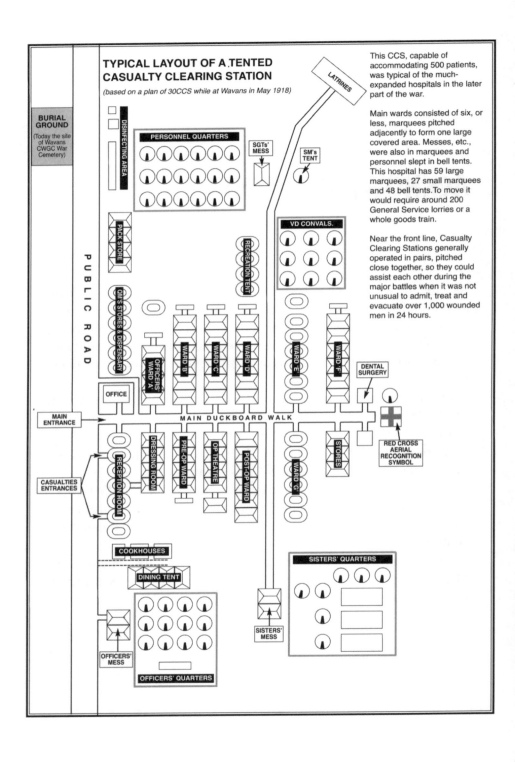

TYPICAL LAYOUT OF A TENTED CASUALTY CLEARING STATION

(based on a plan of 30CCS while at Wavans in May 1918)

LATRINES

BURIAL GROUND

(Today the site of Wavans CWGC War Cemetery)

PUBLIC ROAD

DISINFECTING AREA

PERSONNEL QUARTERS

SGTs' MESS

SM's TENT

PACK STORE

RECREATION TENT

VD CONVALS.

QM'S STORES & DISPENSARY

OFFICERS' WARD 'A'

WARD 'B'

WARD 'C'

WARD 'D'

WARD 'E'

WARD 'F'

DENTAL SURGERY

OFFICE

MAIN ENTRANCE

MAIN DUCKBOARD WALK

RED CROSS AERIAL RECOGNITION SYMBOL

CASUALTIES ENTRANCES

RECEPTION ROOM

DRESSING ROOM

PRE-OP WARD

OP THEATRE

POST-OP WARD

WARD 'G'

STORES

COOKHOUSES

DINING TENT

SISTERS' QUARTERS

SISTERS' MESS

OFFICERS' MESS

OFFICERS' QUARTERS

This CCS, capable of accommodating 500 patients, was typical of the much-expanded hospitals in the later part of the war.

Main wards consisted of six, or less, marquees pitched adjacently to form one large covered area. Messes, etc., were also in marquees and personnel slept in bell tents. This hospital has 59 large marquees, 27 small marquees and 48 bell tents. To move it would require around 200 General Service lorries or a whole goods train.

Near the front line, Casualty Clearing Stations generally operated in pairs, pitched close together, so they could assist each other during the major battles when it was not unusual to admit, treat and evacuate over 1,000 wounded men in 24 hours.

'In nothing do men more nearly approach the gods than in giving health to other men.'
(Cicero)

Chapter 1

THE HAMMER FALLS

THURSDAY 21 MARCH 1918
29TH CASUALTY CLEARING STATION,
ROYAL ARMY MEDICAL CORPS,
GREVILLERS, FRANCE

At 4.40 a.m., Sister M. Aitken of the Australian Army Nursing Service was woken by a violent explosion. Her first thought was that it was an ammunition dump blowing up behind their lines, but when it was followed immediately by two further, and even louder, explosions, she realised with alarm that the British lines were under artillery bombardment from the enemy.

As she hastily got dressed, the shellfire increased in violence and intensity until the explosions merged into an almost continuous roar, defying normal conversation, making the canvas of the tents billow and strain, and the ground on which they were pitched tremble. She had only been here for two days; on Tuesday, together with three other nurses, two Australian and one British, she had joined 29th Casualty Clearing Station (29CCS) to receive their final course of instruction in anaesthesia. Life on the Third Army front had been quiet in recent months and she had expected to receive her tuition in reasonably peaceful and relaxed surroundings. Her last appointment had been at No.1 General Hospital in Étretat, a quiet village on the coast of Normandy and many miles from the frontline. She had never been this close to the battlefields before, let alone come under enemy fire, and she felt a strange mixture of anxiety and elation.

For all she knew, the bombardment might include gas shells; there had been several cases of mustard gas poisoning admitted during the two days she had been in the hospital. So, once dressed, she picked up her gas mask and hurried to the wards through the rows of shaking bell tents and marquees to report to the duty night sister. Throughout the camp, nurses and RAMC orderlies were emerging from tents in varying stages of undress, all intent on getting to their duty stations and finding out what was going on.

When Sister Aitken reached the wards, she saw that the sister-in-charge, Miss F.M. Rice, a senior sister in the Territorial Force Nursing Service (TFNS), was already there, upright, immaculate and imperturbable in her spotless, starched uniform. She was attempting, above the thunder of the bombardment, to converse with Major (Maj.) G.L.K. Pringle of the Royal Army Medical Corps (RAMC), the second-in-command who, only the day before, had been promoted from captain to major. She could not hear what they were saying but, from their gestures, she understood that they were discussing the movement of the patients in the ward.

There were 246 patients in the hospital, which was about the average. As its name implied, the purpose of a casualty clearing station was not to provide long-term care for the sick and wounded, but to inspect and renew dressings which may have been applied hastily at a trench Regimental Aid Post (RAP), or by a stretcher bearer; to undertake urgently needed surgery and to get the patients evacuated from the battle zone and back to a base hospital, well behind the lines, as quickly as possible. It was unusual for a patient to spend more than a day or two in a CCS before being loaded onto an ambulance train for evacuation. Sometimes convoys of motor ambulances, or cars for the walking wounded, would have to be used but, with the poor state of the roads and the crude suspension of motor vehicles at the time, it was a painful form of transport for severely wounded men. The majority of limb amputations were undertaken in the operating theatres of casualty clearing stations and, where transport had to be by motor ambulance, it was not uncommon for a nurse to travel with a patient to hold up what remained of a limb throughout the journey to cushion it from the bumps. For this, among other reasons, casualty clearing stations were usually situated beside, or conveniently close to, a railway line.

As Sister Aitken stood waiting for instructions, there was an explosion even louder than those before; the marquee lurched violently and, with a shriek of ripping canvas and a blast of night air, a piece of shrapnel about the size of a man's hand flew across the ward, missing the head of the sister-in-charge by about 6in. It smashed through the duckboards covering the floor beyond and buried itself a foot deep in the ground. Miss Rice did not flinch and, having made sure that the shrapnel had done no harm to any of her patients or staff, continued her attempted conversation with Major Pringle as if nothing untoward had happened. That, thought Sister Aitken, showed the true professionalism born of a lifetime of discipline and dedication to her calling. She could see by the faces of the patients lying in the beds that the incident had been noticed and that it had had an immediate effect on morale in the ward.

The duty night sister bustled into the ward and, after a hurried consultation with Miss Rice and Major Pringle, beckoned Sister Aitken over and told her to join Sister B. McMunn and Staff Nurse L.A. Stock in the post-surgical ward, where they were already starting to prepare the patients for evacuation.

The enemy bombardment may have come as a surprise to Sister Aitken, but it was no surprise to the commanding officer (CO), Lieutenant Colonel (Lt Col) J.C.G. Carmichael RAMC. A major spring offensive by the enemy had been expected for weeks and it was simply a question of 'when' rather than 'if'. Intelligence sources had reported an increase in troop movements behind the enemy lines in recent weeks and a party of senior German officers had been seen scrutinising the British positions along the Third and Fifth Army fronts. It could only mean that the expected attack was imminent.

The day before, the CO had received warning from headquarters (HQ) that he should be prepared for a move at very short notice. He had immediately ordered all off-duty staff to start packing unused stores and equipment ready for rapid loading. He had not gone to bed that night and had visited every ward in the hospital, giving encouragement to his own men who had also sacrificed a night's sleep to start the packing process.

The British Third Army, guarding a 28-mile section of the Western Front, consisted of twelve Divisions, plus two in reserve. The normal allocation of casualty clearing stations was one for each division and so, consequently, there were twelve CCSs supporting the Third Army. Two of these were further forward than 29CCS — 48CCS at Ytres and 21CCS at Beaulencourt. Both came under heavy shelling on 21 March and were evacuated the same day, leaving 29CCS as the most forward hospital on the Third Army front.

There were two CCSs at Grévillers, just outside the village on the Bapaume road — 29CCS on one side of the road and 3CCS on the other. The two hospitals shared access to the light railway siding from which most of their patients started the long journey back to base hospital. They also shared use of the burial ground for those who would sadly never make the journey.

The initial aim of the enemy bombardment was to disable the British artillery positions behind the lines. The main bulk of the shelling therefore passed over the heads of personnel at 29CCS and, although there were some near misses and some damage to tents and equipment, there were no casualties in the hospital. Further back, where the British gun positions were, the hospitals were less fortunate. At 45CCS at Achiet-le-Grand, less than 2 miles from Grévillers, twenty-five were killed and eleven injured on the morning of the 21st.

At 6 a.m. the sound and feel of the bombardment changed. The veteran soldiers in the wards who had long experience in the frontline knew immediately what was happening: the enemy had stopped bombarding the British artillery positions in the rear and were now shelling the British frontline trenches. The shells were no longer howling overhead; the explosions sounded closer and in the opposite direction. The staff at 29CCS knew that the casualties would soon start arriving.

At 7 a.m. the first men arrived – straggling columns of walking wounded, hobbling on shattered legs and supported by mates on either side; heads swathed in bandages with ugly red stains seeping through; men clutching bloody field dressings to gaping wounds in chests and abdomens, or nursing shattered arms in makeshift slings. Then came the more seriously injured – crying out in pain or moaning gently in morphine-induced demi-peace; borne on stretchers carried by tin-hatted soldiers with Red Cross armbands.

The casualties were met as they arrived and the triage sisters assessed their condition. Those in need of critical surgery joined the stream for the two operating theatres where the surgical teams were hard at work. In the first theatre, the surgeons Captains Littlejohn and Mowat-Biggs, and in the second Captains Roe and Walker, supported by their experienced teams of theatre sisters and orderlies, worked throughout the day without a break.

In other treatment areas, doctors, nurses and orderlies applied splints, dressed wounds and did what they could to ease the pain of injured and badly shocked men. In another area, seriously wounded men with no hope of recovery were made as comfortable as possible, their final moments often eased by the presence of a nurse to talk to them and hold their hands, or by comforting words and spiritual reassurance from one of the three chaplains attached to the hospital. By 10 a.m. the fifteen wards of the hospital were almost full and stretchers were waiting on the ground outside the reception tent.

At 3CCS across the road, the position was just the same: their wards were full and rows of stretchers were piling up on the ground outside the reception area. Though all the medical staff were working flat out, the influx of casualties was too great for them to keep up. The sister-in-charge at 3CCS, Miss W.M. Gedye, a regular officer in Queen Alexandra's Imperial Military Nursing Service (QAIMNS), sent a messenger to Miss Rice at 29CCS asking whether she could help out with nurses or beds? But their situation was exactly the same.

At 7 a.m. the enemy bombardment eased, but the influx of injured men did not abate. Then, at 9.35 a.m., 3,500 enemy mortars opened fire on the British frontline, followed by, five minutes later, by waves of German infantry pouring across no-man's-land to the British trenches. They were met by determined British soldiers with Lee Enfield .303 rifles with sword bayonets fixed. The carnage on both sides was appalling. The triage sisters in the reception area noted that the nature of wounds was changing: the majority of earlier casualties had been as a result of shrapnel from artillery shelling; now the admissions showed signs of violent, hand-to-hand fighting, with gunshot wounds the predominant injuries. Similarly, as the earlier casualties had tended to be gunners from the beleaguered Royal Artillery gun emplacements behind the lines, the admissions now were largely from the frontline

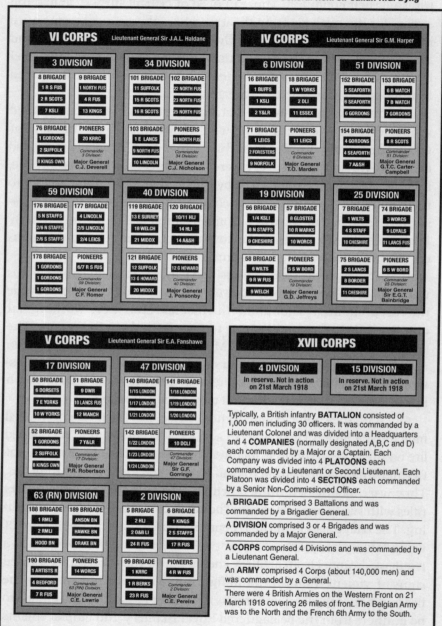

THE BRITISH THIRD ARMY

at 21 March 1918
General Hon. Sir Julian H.G. Byng

VI CORPS — Lieutenant General Sir J.A.L. Haldane

3 DIVISION

8 BRIGADE	9 BRIGADE
1 R S FUS	1 NORTH FUS
2 R SCOTS	4 R FUS
7 KSLI	13 KINGS

76 BRIGADE	PIONEERS
1 GORDONS	20 KRRC
2 SUFFOLK	
8 KINGS OWN	Commander 3 Division: Major General C.J. Deverell

34 DIVISION

101 BRIGADE	102 BRIGADE
11 SUFFOLK	22 NORTH FUS
15 R SCOTS	23 NORTH FUS
16 R SCOTS	25 NORTH FUS

103 BRIGADE	PIONEERS
1 E LANCS	18 NORTH FUS
9 NORTH FUS	
10 LINCOLN	Commander 34 Division: Major General C.J. Nicholson

59 DIVISION

176 BRIGADE	177 BRIGADE
5 N STAFFS	4 LINCOLN
2/6 N STAFFS	2/5 LINCOLN
2/6 S STAFFS	2/4 LEICS

178 BRIGADE	PIONEERS
1 GORDONS	6/7 R S FUS
1 GORDONS	
1 GORDONS	Commander 59 Division: Major General C.F. Romer

40 DIVISION

119 BRIGADE	120 BRIGADE
13 E SURREY	10/11 HLI
18 WELCH	14 HLI
21 MIDDX	14 A&SH

121 BRIGADE	PIONEERS
12 SUFFOLK	12 G HOWARD
13 G HOWARD	
20 MIDDX	Commander 40 Division: Major General J. Ponsonby

IV CORPS — Lieutenant General Sir G.M. Harper

6 DIVISION

16 BRIGADE	18 BRIGADE
1 BUFFS	1 W YORKS
1 KSLI	2 DLI
2 Y&LR	11 ESSEX

71 BRIGADE	PIONEERS
1 LEICS	11 LEICS
2 FORESTERS	
9 NORFOLK	Commander 6 Division: Major General T.O. Marden

51 DIVISION

152 BRIGADE	153 BRIGADE
5 SEAFORTH	6 B WATCH
6 SEAFORTH	7 B WATCH
6 GORDONS	7 GORDONS

154 BRIGADE	PIONEERS
4 GORDONS	8 R SCOTS
4 SEAFORTH	
7 A&SH	Commander 51 Division: Major General G.T.C. Carter-Campbell

19 DIVISION

56 BRIGADE	57 BRIGADE
1/4 KSLI	8 GLOSTER
8 N STAFFS	10 R WARKS
9 CHESHIRE	10 WORCS

58 BRIGADE	PIONEERS
6 WILTS	5 S W BORD
9 R W FUS	
9 WELCH	Commander 19 Division: Major General G.D. Jeffreys

25 DIVISION

7 BRIGADE	74 BRIGADE
1 WILTS	3 WORCS
4 S STAFF	9 LOYALS
10 CHESHIRE	11 LANCS FUS

75 BRIGADE	PIONEERS
2 S LANCS	6 S W BORD
8 BORDER	
11 CHESHIRE	Commander 25 Division: Major General Sir E.G.T. Bainbridge

V CORPS — Lieutenant General Sir E.A. Fanshawe

17 DIVISION

50 BRIGADE	51 BRIGADE
6 DORSETS	9 DWR
7 E YORKS	10 LANCS FUS
10 W YORKS	12 MANCH

52 BRIGADE	PIONEERS
1 GORDONS	7 Y&LR
2 SUFFOLK	
8 KINGS OWN	Commander 17 Division: Major General P.R. Robertson

47 DIVISION

140 BRIGADE	141 BRIGADE
1/15 LONDON	1/18 LONDON
1/17 LONDON	1/19 LONDON
1/21 LONDON	1/20 LONDON

142 BRIGADE	PIONEERS
1/22 LONDON	10 DCLI
1/23 LONDON	
1/24 LONDON	Commander 47 Division: Major General Sir G.F. Gorringe

63 (RN) DIVISION

188 BRIGADE	189 BRIGADE
1 RMLI	ANSON BN
2 RMLI	HAWKE BN
HOOD BN	DRAKE BN

190 BRIGADE	PIONEERS
1 ARTISTS R	14 WORCS
4 BEDFORD	
7 R FUS	Commander 63 (RN) Division: Major General C.E. Lawrie

2 DIVISION

5 BRIGADE	6 BRIGADE
2 HLI	1 KINGS
2 O&B LI	2 S STAFFS
24 R FUS	17 R FUS

99 BRIGADE	PIONEERS
1 KRRC	4 R W FUS
1 R BERKS	
23 R FUS	Commander 2 Division: Major General C.E. Pereira

XVII CORPS

4 DIVISION	15 DIVISION
In reserve. Not in action on 21st March 1918	In reserve. Not in action on 21st March 1918

Typically, a British infantry **BATTALION** consisted of 1,000 men including 30 officers. It was commanded by a Lieutenant Colonel and was divided into a Headquarters and 4 **COMPANIES** (normally designated A,B,C and D) each commanded by a Major or a Captain. Each Company was divided into 4 **PLATOONS** each commanded by a Lieutenant or Second Lieutenant. Each Platoon was divided into 4 **SECTIONS** each commanded by a Senior Non-Commissioned Officer.

A **BRIGADE** comprised 3 Battalions and was commanded by a Brigadier General.

A **DIVISION** comprised 3 or 4 Brigades and was commanded by a Major General.

A **CORPS** comprised 4 Divisions and was commanded by a Lieutenant General.

An **ARMY** comprised 4 Corps (about 140,000 men) and was commanded by a General.

There were 4 British Armies on the Western Front on 21 March 1918 covering 26 miles of front. The Belgian Army was to the North and the French 6th Army to the South.

For full regimental names see index.

infantry battalions of the 6th and 51st (Highland) Divisions such as the 2nd Durham Light Infantry, 1st King's Shropshire Light Infantry, 1st Leicesters or 4th Seaforths.

At 29CCS the pressure of patients waiting for amputations and major surgery was so intense that, by noon, the two operating theatres clearly could not cope. It was vital for these men to receive surgery here at the CCS; without it, wounds could turn gangrenous on the journey and patients would be die en route to the base hospital.

So the CO ordered the post-operative ward to be prepared as an emergency theatre and detailed two of his medical officers, Captain (Capt.) Dill and Lt Brockwell, to stand in as an emergency surgical team. Miss Rice detailed four nurses and four orderlies to support them. With two more operating tables in action, the queues for surgery slowly shortened.

Outside the camp, Sergeant (Sgt) E.H. Boswell RAMC worked tirelessly to supervise the smooth running of the motor convoys, the queues of stretcher bearers bringing casualties from the front and those which were transporting the wounded who had already been treated in the hospital to No.7 Ambulance Train (AT), which stood in the siding next to the camp. When full, it would evacuate the casualties to the base hospital at Doullens. At the siding, Sgt J. Orr RAMC checked the patients onto the train and marked off their names on his dispersals list.

On board the train, nurses and orderlies received the patients and made them as comfortable as possible in the rows of three-tiered cots lining the sides of the carriages. Getting badly wounded patients into the top cots was one of the jobs the nurses liked least: it was almost impossible to transfer a badly wounded man from a stretcher to a top cot without causing him acute pain and the upper tier was, therefore, whenever possible, reserved for less serious cases.

The ambulance train had its own permanent staff of doctors, nurses and orderlies, messes for the medical staff, cookhouses to prepare food for staff and patients, and to provide a continuous supply of hot water for clinical purposes, a pharmacy, a stores wagon and a tiled, emergency operating theatre which could, in extreme circumstances, be used for procedures when the train was moving. A typical ambulance train had sixteen carriages and accommodated about 400 patients in wards of thirty-six cots. The centre tier of cots could be folded up to take sitting cases on the bottom row.

As soon as the train was full, a locomotive arrived and pulled the carriages out towards the main line. Within half an hour another ambulance train, 38AT, had drawn into the siding and the loading of patients started again.

The casualties arriving from the frontline brought gloomy news: the enemy was in immense strength and was breaking through all along the British lines. At 1 p.m. the CO received orders from the HQ of the Director Medical Services (DMS) to clear all patients from 29CCS and prepare to hand over the site to a field ambulance (FA). Admissions ceased and casualties were diverted to 3CCS across the road. In the course of the day, 29CCS had admitted 949 patients on top of the 246 already in the hospital before hostilities started. The admissions included twelve mustard gas cases, seven Indians of the 41st Indian Labour Company and one wounded French civilian who had been unlucky enough to get in the way of the conflict. The two ambulance trains evacuated 710 patients and a further 451 were transferred to 56CCS at Dernancourt (known to the British as Edgehill).

Then, as dusk fell, a sad cortege of orderlies and stretcher bearers, accompanied by the CO and Revd R. Holme of the Royal Army Chaplains Department (RAChD), made its way to the burial ground beside the camp where the bodies of sixteen brave men who had died in the hospital during the day were laid to rest: two gunners of the Royal Garrison Artillery, Corporal (Cpl) C. Ward (95 Siege Battery) and Gunner (Gnr) F. Bridger (131 Siege Battery); two gunners of the Royal Field Artillery (RFA), Gnr W.W. Cornes and Gnr A.J. Thomson; three men of the 51st Battalion, Machine Gun Corps, Private (Pte) E. Wood, Pte W. Brotherton and Pte J. Ritchie; one Royal Engineer, Cpl R.A. Howes; seven infantry soldiers, Pte J. Brown (25th Northumberland Fusiliers), Pte T. Capper (Cheshires), Pte M. Gillingham (King's), Pte J.S. Hardman (Durham Light Infantry), Pte H. Kelvert (King's Shropshire Light Infantry), Pte F. Smart (2nd/4th Leicestershires), and Pte G. Gemmel (4th Seaforth Highlanders). Pte Gemmel had been admitted unconscious with serious gunshot wounds to the head; he had no dog tag and absolutely no kit with him from which his army number could be obtained. The fact was noted in the hospital records and it was left to the Graves Registration (GR) Units to later obtain his details from regimental records.

The final burial was undertaken in a separate plot. The victim was Pte Mohinder Singh of the 41st Indian Labour Company. He was a Sikh from the Punjab. Though his language and customs were unknown to anyone present, army chaplains were dedicated to the service of all religions and denominations, and Reverend (Revd) Holme, though a United Board chaplain (belonging to the Baptist, United Reformed or Congregational Churches) accorded the burial exactly the same respect and dignity that the others had received.

Back at 29CCS the frenzied work continued to pack up stores and equipment for evacuation. The tents of the camp were already coming down. At this stage of its existence, 29CCS was housed in forty-one marquees and thirty bell tents. To transport the hospital under normal circumstances would require twenty-seven horse-drawn general service wagons or twelve 3-ton motor lorries. It occupied a site of about 300 sq yds.

The hospital was now cleared of all its patients, with the exception of eighteen 'venereal convalescents'. These men, who had paid the price for straying from the paths of virtue with one of the many French ladies of the night who plied their trade in the rest areas behind the lines, were technically under open arrest in the hospital, but in practice formed a cheery, willing and able-bodied labour force to assist with the many duties around the camp – digging ditches and latrines, loading stores and equipment and, on this day, pulling down tents and bundling them up ready for transport. Work continued into the night, with every member of the hospital staff involved. This would be the CO's second night without sleep and none of his staff would go to bed either.

At 3CCS across the road, the pressure had never eased. With 29CCS now closed for admissions, the workload of the already hard-pressed doctors and nurses was doubled, and there was no alternative but to divert all arrivals, other than those obviously requiring urgent surgical attention, to Edgehill. The rows of stretchers outside the admissions area were increasing all the time and the stream of ambulances arriving to transport them could not keep pace with the volume.

At 3 a.m. on Friday 22 March, the CO received orders to evacuate 29CCS and to take command of 3CCS over the road. Nine lorries were loaded with the equipment and stores for a 300-bed unit, and the tents and other equipment were loaded onto an empty ammunition train, which had just unloaded shells for the British artillery batteries at Grévillers. The 29CCS equipment took up three-quarters of the train, leaving just enough room for the personnel of 3CCS who were in a state of complete exhaustion, having worked without a break since 7 a.m. the previous day. Since 29CCS had been ordered to close for admissions, and 48CCS at Ytres and 21CCS at Beaulencourt had been evacuated in the teeth of the enemy's advance, 3CCS had taken the full burden of casualties on the Third Army front. Since the previous day, their operating theatres and dressing stations had been in continuous use, and they had admitted 3,627 wounded and 300 sick.

At 5 a.m. orders were received for the nursing sisters from 29CCS to be evacuated to the safety of No.3 Canadian Hospital at Doullens. They had done magnificent work under dangerous and stressful conditions. For those who had not served in an advanced unit before, such as Sister Aitken, it had been a baptism of fire and an experience they would never forget. Every lady had acquitted herself with distinction and Miss Rice had every reason to be proud of her girls who had left in a convoy of cars by 7 a.m. After their departure, the site of 29CCS was handed over to 1/3 Highland Field Ambulance (51st Highland Division) and Lt Col Carmichael and the remainder of his staff moved across the road to take control of the massive backlog of wounded at 3CCS. All the wards were now full and the stretchers were stacked in rows in the open. Wounded men were still arriving in there hundreds and the continuous convoy of cars and ambulances were not sufficient to keep pace with the casualties.

Ambulance trains could not be brought into the Grévillers siding as the railway found itself under shellfire. The sound of battle was getting closer and closer, and the British artillery batteries were in full song. One battery of heavy artillery had opened fire right beside the hospital and the noise was deafening. The battery commander sent a concerned message to the CO of the hospital, warning him that the enemy was very close; he did not need to be told.

In the late afternoon, Lt E.R. Chamness, an American loan officer of the Medical Officer Reserve Corps (MORC), together with twenty-seven RAMC soldiers, arrived for duty from No.16 Field Ambulance. The Colonel was delighted to see them – he needed all the hands he could get. Then, as dusk fell, enemy aircraft came over and started to bomb the

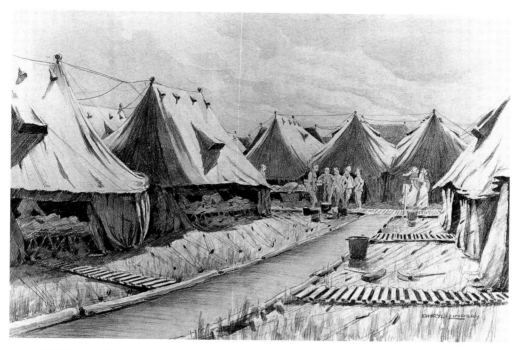

001 A Casualty Clearing Station on the Western Front. Daryl Lindsay © Wellcome Library, London

002 Collecting the wounded from a battlefield. Daryl Lindsay © Wellcome Library, London

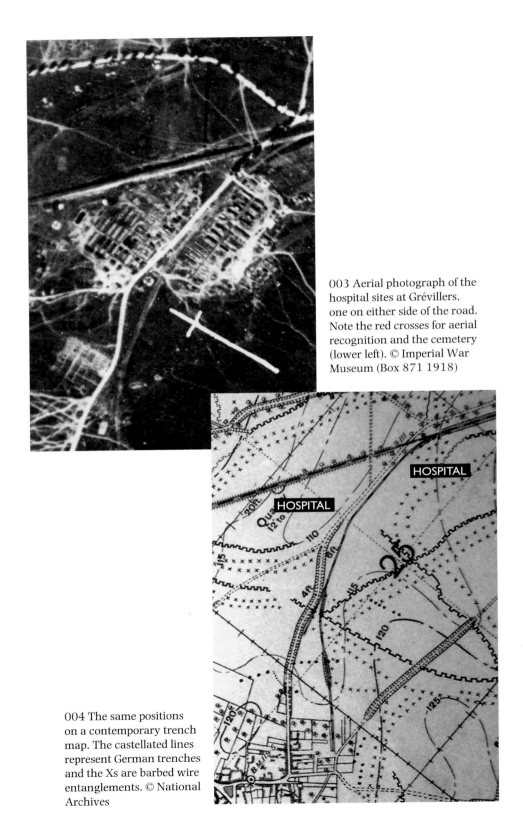

003 Aerial photograph of the hospital sites at Grévillers, one on either side of the road. Note the red crosses for aerial recognition and the cemetery (lower left). © Imperial War Museum (Box 871 1918)

HOSPITAL

HOSPITAL

004 The same positions on a contemporary trench map. The castellated lines represent German trenches and the Xs are barbed wire entanglements. © National Archives

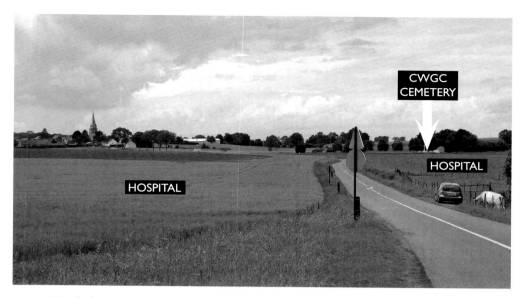

CWGC CEMETERY

HOSPITAL

HOSPITAL

005 The hospital sites at Grévillers today with Grévillers village and church in the background (left) and the CWGC cemetery (right). The hospital railway siding would have run roughly along the dividing line of the short and long grass in the field on the left.

006 29 Casualty Clearing Station at Grévillers on 21 March 1918, the first day of the big German offensive. The wards in 29CCS and 3CCS are overflowing and the ambulance trains cannot arrive quickly enough to deal with the massive intake of casualties. Here, patients on stretchers lie in rows beside the railway siding waiting for the next train to evacuate them to a base hospital. By noon the following day, the two hospitals will have admitted more than 4,000 wounded men. © Army Medical Services Museum

007 Grévillers British War Cemetery in the early 1920s with the wooden crosses still in place. © Commonwealth War Graves Commission

008 The Cemetery today.

009 No.33 Ambulance Train stands on the hospital siding at Grévillers on 27 November 1917. The following day it left for base hospital with 99 patients from 29CCS. The main Achiet-Marcoing railway line is in the foreground. © Imperial War museum (Q47147)

010 The same view today. The main line is now derelict and the hospital siding has been removed. Inset: The derelict main line.

011 An Advanced Dressing Station close behind the frontline. © Wellcome Library, London

012 A Regimental Aid Post in the trenches. © Wellcome Library, London

013 'Nightfall'. A poignant picture of blinded and partially blinded men, each with a hand on the shoulder of the man in front for guidance, in a shuffling queue for treatment at a Casualty Clearing Station. © Wellcome Library, London

014 German prisoners assist British stretcher bearers to gather the wounded on a battlefield for transportation to a Field Ambulance or Casualty Clearing Station. © Wellcome Library, London

015 Casualty Collection Point on a Somme battlefield. © Army Medical Services Museum

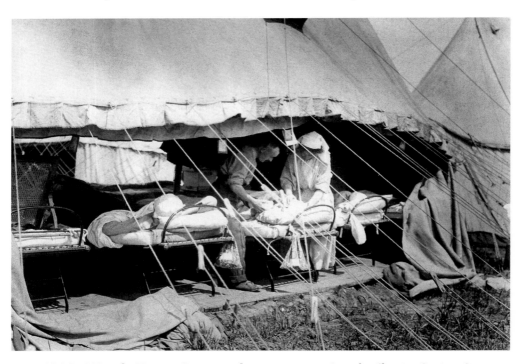

016 An MO and a Nursing Sister attend to a patient in a Casualty Clearing Station. © Army Medical Services Museum

hospital, despite the huge Red Cross flag pinned out on the ground for identification. The CO sent a message to HQ saying the position was grave; unless the supply of cars and ambulances could be sent in far greater numbers, it was inevitable that the enemy would overrun the position before all the wounded could be evacuated. The flow of cars was increased and, gradually, as the night progressed, the queues of patients lessened.

By 2 a.m. on the 23rd, there were only six patients remaining in the hospital and the CO received orders to evacuate all personnel immediately. By 3.30 a.m. all officers and men had been loaded onto a goods train but, although the line was no longer under enemy fire, an enormous British railway gun, mounted on two carriages, was now blocking the way and the train could not leave. Eventually it got away and arrived at Edgehill at 7 a.m.

The CO and the quartermaster (QM), Lt J. Davies RAMC, stayed behind to ensure there were no stragglers and to recover any equipment that could be saved. They left by car and arrived at Edgehill at 6 a.m., having gone via HQ so the Colonel could report on the position with the two hospitals. He had not slept for three consecutive nights and on arrival at Edgehill he lay down fully clothed on the floor of a filthy tent, sleeping deeply and undisturbed for two and a half hours.

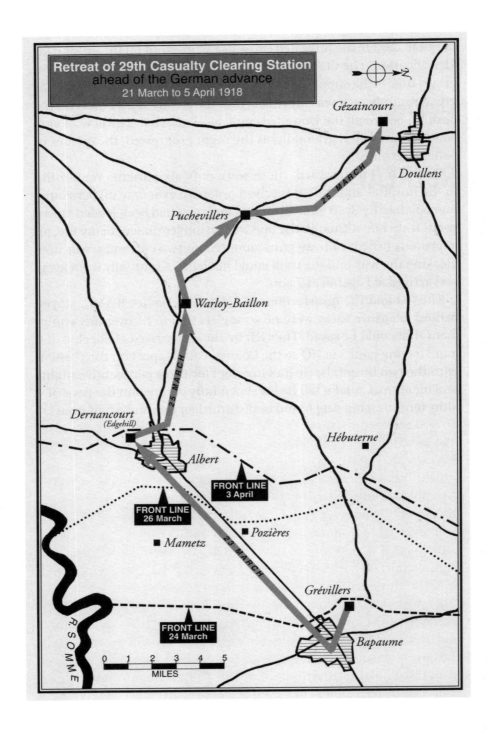

Retreat of 29th Casualty Clearing Station
ahead of the German advance
21 March to 5 April 1918

Gézaincourt

Doullens

25 MARCH

Puchevillers

Warloy-Baillon

25 MARCH

Dernancourt
(Edgehill)

Hébuterne

Albert

FRONT LINE
3 April

FRONT LINE
26 March

Mametz

Pozières

23 MARCH

FRONT LINE
24 March

Grévillers

Bapaume

R. SOMME

0   1   2   3   4   5
MILES

Chapter 2

RETREAT

At 8.30 a.m. the Colonel was woken by his batman; orders had come through from DMS for the 29CCS equipment to be unloaded from the ammunition train and loaded onto another goods train which had arrived at Edgehill the previous day. Having ensured that his men had had some hot tea and a rudimentary breakfast, he got them started on this onerous task.

At this time there were five casualty clearing stations temporarily assembled at Edgehill – 56CCS, which had been there since before the attack; 3CCS and 29CCS had just arrived from Grévillers; 21CCS had been evacuated from Beaulencourt and 48CCS from Ytres. Together they formed a vast tented township north-west of the village of Dernancourt on both sides of the Millencourt road. There was considerable confusion, each unit having managed to save a differing amount of its stores and equipment, and having succeeded in retaining differing levels of personnel, all of whom were suffering from acute fatigue and unsure of what their duties were supposed to be. In the meantime, the flow of casualties had not abated and the thousands of wounded from the whole southern sector of the Third Army front were now converging on Edgehill. The senior officer present was the CO of 3CCS,

35

Lt Col Rae RAMC, who was appointed Senior Medical Officer (SMO) at Edgehill and set about organising a rota for admissions and attempted to bring some sort of order to the chaos.

By noon 29CCS had finished unloading and reloading its equipment as ordered. The next order, to immediately unload it all and to load it onto another train to be handed over to 21CCS, which had lost most of its own equipment, was therefore received with some dismay. It was hard to bear for the men of 29CCS, who had worked extremely hard without sleep for two days and nights to pack up their equipment and who had managed to save more than any other CCS. But orders were orders and, albeit with some understandable grumbling and a deep sense of injustice, they set to work again.

In view of the state of fatigue of all the medical staff, Lt Col Rae decided upon a rota system under which the personnel of each unit worked in shifts a few hours at a time, relieving each other in turn. 29CCS took over from 48CCS in the afternoon and admitted 1,055 wounded during the next eight hours.

Although the soldiers in the British frontline knew they had been attacked by a vastly superior force, they were not to know just how vastly superior it had been until much later. In fact, on Thursday 21 March, seventy-six German divisions had attacked the twenty-nine under-strength divisions of the British Third and Fifth Armies; a superiority in men of nearly three to one, while the Germans had 6,000 guns to the British 2,800.

Field Marshal (FM) Sir Douglas Haig, the British commander-in-chief, certain that a massive attack was imminent, had pleaded with the prime minister, David Lloyd George, to release sufficient men from the reserve in Britain to bring his divisions up to strength. Some divisions were deficient of up to 2,000 men and Haig needed only 150,000 men out of a total of 650,000 in Britain who were fully trained and ready for immediate deployment overseas. Lloyd George consistently refused and a bitter political conflict between the two men ensued.

In spite of the fact that every intelligence source available to the British and French commanders had warned that a major German attack on the Western Front was imminent, Lloyd George would not believe it, clinging to the naive belief that Allied efforts should be concentrated in the east against Germany's ally Turkey – a concept which, naturally enough, with the north of their country occupied by the enemy, was completely unacceptable to the French.

Allied losses during the previous year had certainly been appalling, with the British offensives at Arras, Passchendaele and Cambrai contributing to some 850,000 casualties. The French losses had been around 600,000, at least 100,000 of which were attributable to the disastrous Nivelle Spring Offensive, during which French medical support had entirely broken down and large sections of the French Army had mutinied.

Stunned by these losses, the British prime minister had done all in his power to freeze the supply of troops to the Western Front in the belief that it would minimise casualties, even to the extent of deliberately misleading the House of Commons as to the strength of British troops on the Western Front compared with the previous year. On 14 March, one week before the German attack, Haig, in desperation, had travelled to London in a last ditch attempt to get Lloyd George to understand the situation and release reinforcements. He would not be persuaded, however, and the meeting ended in considerable acrimony. Haig returned to France and warned his commanders that they must prepare for a very strong attack along a 50-mile front within the next few days. This, he warned them, must be met by their under-strength divisions, which would not, now, be reinforced from Britain.

It had apparently not occurred to Lloyd George that the best way to minimise British casualties might have been to ensure that the defenders were adequately manned to meet the attack.

As far as the Germans were concerned, there had been little dissension between the views of the politicians and the military. General (Gen.) Erich von Ludendorff, who had earned a reputation as a field commander of genius on the Eastern Front, was determined that Germany should launch a massive spring offensive in the west. Russia had collapsed into revolution, releasing eighty German divisions for the Western Front. With a significant superiority in men and guns, this would be Germany's very last chance for a decisive, war-winning victory before the Americans entered the war and changed the entire balance of power. It was now or never, and despite the fact that Germany was effectively bankrupt, and her starving citizens back home were eating cats and dogs and bread made from sawdust, all the nation's remaining resources would be sunk into this mighty, last-ditch endeavour.

Any such opposition to the plan had soon been steamrolled by Ludendorff with a mixture of bullying and threats, and Germany was set on course for the Ludendorff Offensive. Aware of the weakness of the undermanned British divisions, the delicate state of morale among the French troops and the intrinsic vulnerability of an area where two armies under separate command adjoined, the strategic aim of Operation Michael was to smash through the British lines, with the heaviest emphasis of the attack on the southern sector of the Fifth Army at its junction with the French Sixth Army. Ludendorff was confident that his legions could do this without difficulty and would then wheel north-west to encircle the British position at Arras, which, once taken, would herald the beginning of the end of the British Expeditionary Force (BEF). France would then negotiate a peace and the whole business would be tied up before America had a chance to flood the Western Front with hundreds of thousands of fresh, well-equipped and provisioned soldiers, the arrival of whom, Ludendorff and everyone else realised, would spell the end of Germany's chances.

Such was the confusion at Edgehill on 23 March that, at one point, DMS appears to have been unaware, or had forgotten, which casualty clearing stations were there. In the morning, all CCSs were ordered to close down and evacuate. However, 48CCS was ordered to reopen and it was in their tents and with their equipment that the personnel of all five units were taking it in turns to deal with the incessant flow of casualties. The following day, the order to close and evacuate the other units was countermanded. The personnel of 29CCS watched ruefully as their erstwhile equipment, now in the care of 21CCS, pulled out of Edgehill. They were not to be reunited with it; 21CCS went to Corbie, then on to Amiens and the two units never met again.

The medical staff of 29CCS worked on admissions until 1 a.m. on Sunday 24 March. Lt Col Carmichael got to bed at 2 a.m. and enjoyed the luxury of six hours sleep before being woken at 8 a.m. to speak to HQ on the field telephone. He was ordered to return immediately to Grévillers to assess and report on the condition of the roads, and the feasibility of salvaging any of the tents left behind by 3CCS. He left Edgehill by car with one of his Army Service Corps (ASC) drivers at 8.25 a.m.

It soon became apparent, however, that it would be a long journey. The road was solid with men, vehicles and guns retiring from the frontline. From time to time the slow moving queues would come to a complete halt as some incident ahead blocked the way. The streets of Albert were solid with congested traffic parked and awaiting orders. The driver found a detour around the town, only to be stopped again at La Boiselle where a party of pioneers were working to repair a huge crater in the road. Some of the traffic, impatient to get through, had taken to the fields on either side of the obstruction. Several had become bogged down in soft ground and their crews were struggling to get them moving. A little further on, a huge heavy artillery gun had overturned and was blocking the road. The traffic had been stopped for twenty minutes while a team of horses from the same battery, which was further ahead, returned along the congested road to assist in righting the gun.

The men on foot looked tired and dirty. Many were supporting walking wounded and a few were carrying stretcher cases who had not been able to get a ride on a lorry. They, of course, would all be heading for the hospital camp at Edgehill. The cheerful air and light-footed deportment which the Colonel had so often witnessed in fresh troops marching to the front was not to be seen in the faces of these men; their's were expressions of hopelessness and defeat. As a result of the British government's decision not to send reinforcements, every man here had had to attempt to repel, on average, three enemy soldiers each.

At 10.55 a.m., after a two-and-a-half-hour journey, the Colonel reached the old hospital site at Grévillers. The No.41 Field Ambulance was under heavy fire and was attempting to leave. There could be no question of trying to salvage any of the tents and equipment, much of which had been damaged by enemy shellfire. After a hurried consultation with the unit's CO, the Colonel returned to Edgehill and, by the evening of the same day, the Germans had taken Bapaume and advanced as far as Grévillers.

In the afternoon of the 24th an order was received from DMS Third Army, effectively instructing all medical units at Edgehill to close and evacuate immediately:

> ... 56 and 48CCSs are to close at once and hand over cases to 3CCS together with buildings. No more cases will be taken in. All will be

diverted to Doullens. Two CCSs will pack up at once. 3CCS will evacuate all cases by AT as speedily as possible and then pack up.

The order made no mention of 21CCS and 29CCS, almost as if DMS had forgotten they were there. However, the medical service was critically overloaded and the HQ staff under extreme pressure, so a degree of inconsistency is understandable. As the Official History observes, DMS clearly intended Edgehill to be closed immediately and for no more wounded to be sent there.

During the afternoon, personnel from 48CCS left by train without their equipment. 29CCS continued to operate on their premises, admitting 508 patients in four hours and clearing the bulk of the seriously wounded in two ambulance trains. By 9 p.m. there were 1,420 patients left at Edgehill and, although they had been classified as 'walking wounded', many had serious injuries and should have been stretcher cases under normal circumstances.

Despite continual pleas to HQ for an ambulance train and more cars, Lt Col Carmichael was told there was no chance of another AT getting into Edgehill, nor of a supply of cars sufficient to evacuate the large number of casualties. He was ordered to divide the patients into two groups: those who could walk about 5 miles and those who could not, who were to be left behind with one medical officer and a few men to be captured by the enemy. The Colonel gave this unsavoury task to Sgt Orr who, with a group of orderlies, set about dividing the patients into two separate columns. At last it was done.

Sgt John Orr was one of the Colonel's most trusted non-commissioned officers (NCOs). He was the holder of the Military Service Medal (MSM) and Bar, having shown great courage and presence of mind following a dreadful train accident at Gézaincourt in 1916, in which many men had perished. Sgt Orr had fought the flames unceasingly in his efforts to extricate wounded men from the inferno and there were several who owed their lives to his courage. The look on his face when he appeared at the flap of the CO's tent at 9 p.m. indicated that there was trouble. He explained to the Colonel that the men had got wind of the fact that the 'non-walkers' were to be left behind and had refused to remain in two separate columns.

The CO went outside and saw that the mass of men had discarded the barriers between the two columns and had deliberately intermingled. Seriously wounded patients clung round the necks of fitter companions on either side. One group had discovered a supply of stretchers in one of the tents and was passing them out to the others who were gently loading men with grievous injuries onto them, often covering them with their own mud-stained greatcoats. There was no shortage of volunteers for stretcher bearers. One young soldier, his head swathed in blood-soaked bandages and supporting one side of a badly wounded comrade, caught the Colonel's eye and said, 'It's alright, Sir. We'll look after 'em. No need to leave anyone behind, Sir.'

At 9.30 p.m., to the delight of all, an empty ammunition train stopped at the hospital site. The Colonel designated it a temporary ambulance train (TAT) and ordered all the remaining patients to be loaded onto it for immediate evacuation under the care of two MOs, Capt. Dill and Lt Brockwell, and eleven RAMC men. As the patients boarded the train, smiles had returned to tired, dirty faces and cheery banter was heard again on the lips of men who in Britain had been herdsmen and builders' labourers, but who now loaded their seriously wounded companions with all the care and tenderness of experienced nurses. The train left Edgehill at 10 p.m. with the strains of 'When this Bloomin War is over...' sung to the tune of 'What a Friend we have in Jesus', competing with the sighs and hisses of the little locomotive towing them to safety.

The Colonel later wrote to his wife:

When their backs are truly against the wall, there is a sublime stoicism in our soldiers that is the only joyous thing about this awful conflict. If I live to be a hundred I will never be more deeply moved than by the selfless heroism shown that night by these remarkable young men.

The personnel of 29CCS, the last medical unit remaining at Edgehill, were ordered to board some empty railway trucks standing on the line and told that an engine would be sent to take them away. The exhausted men installed themselves, several of them falling into a deep sleep on the floor of the filthy trucks within minutes. They were soon awakened as enemy aircraft appeared overhead and bombs started dropping around them. They tumbled from the trucks and took whatever shelter they could find beside the line. When the aircraft left, they boarded the trucks again, only to be roused half an hour later by the same sequence of events.

At 1 a.m. on Monday 25 March, the CO received fresh orders: the railway line had been damaged in several places by the enemy bombers and no locomotive could be sent. All personnel were to detrain and march the 21 miles to Doullens. The Colonel wrote:

> The men's behaviour was simply splendid; not a murmur, not a grumble. We were all dead on our feet and none of us had had a square meal for four days and then to embark upon a 21-mile march in the dead of night!

The NCOs got them formed up in threes and they set off on their long trek, the light from an almost full moon casting shadows of the skeletons of trees robbed of their flesh by the continuous bombardment of artillery. Little remained of the people who farmed these lands in less troubled times. They had almost all taken themselves off to relatives in safer parts of France, their farmhouses and outbuildings now used as billets for soldiers, their fields now serving as picket lines and gun parks.

The column of tired men crossed the main Amiens road, which was still congested by retiring guns and lorries, their acetylene headlamps forming a glowing trail which wound away into the distance towards Albert. They passed through the villages of Laviéville and Hénencourt until, at 4 a.m., they reached Warloy-Baillon, where they were stopped by a despatch rider with orders that they should halt there and await further orders.

One of the officers had been in this village before and told the CO that there was a French hospital hospice where they might be able to shelter for a few hours. They found their way to it and roused the matron, who was sympathetic but explained that the whole building was already full to capacity. However, there was a barn in the grounds where the soldiers could sleep and the officers could spend what remained of the night on the floor of the porter's lodge. They woke three hours later, stiff with cold and famished.

The CO sent a party of men to scavenge for food, but all they could find for sale was a few biscuits and some dry tea. They bought all they could and the matron gave them access to the kitchens for boiling water, so every man had a couple of biscuits and a mug of hot tea; for many it was the most welcome cup of tea they would ever enjoy. But this was far from adequate. The QM, Lt Davies, had gone ahead of the unit on a lorry to arrange for provisions when they reached Doullens. The Colonel now sent a messenger ahead on a bicycle he had requisitioned to instruct the QM to send rations, a Sawyers stove and fuel to Puchevillers, the next village on their march.

The unit left Warloy-Baillon at 8 a.m. and arrived in Puchevillers at 11 a.m. Two hours later, to cheers of delight and relief from the hungry men, a lorry arrived with rations and a stove and everyone enjoyed the first square meal they had had since the previous Thursday – bully beef, bread and butter, and hot tea. Their hunger sated, the men lay down in a wood at the edge of the village and slept.

The Colonel, though thoroughly overtired, found he could not sleep. He was filthy dirty, with two days growth of beard and, being a man of meticulous personal cleanliness, felt extremely uncomfortable. Two months previously the Royal Flying Corps (RFC) and the Royal Naval Air Service (RNAS) had combined to become the Royal Air Force (RAF) and this new service had an airfield and flying school just outside Puchevillers. The Colonel walked to the officers' mess where one of the young pilots chivalrously offered him his room for a shave and a bath in a hand basin. Thus refreshed and with a clean pair of socks, the Colonel returned to the wood where his men were sleeping. He let them sleep on until 4 p.m., then had them roused, formed up and the march recommenced.

Chapter 3

CONSOLIDATION

MONDAY 25 MARCH 1918
29TH CASUALTY CLEARING STATION,
ROYAL ARMY MEDICAL CORPS AT PUCHEVILLERS, FRANCE
ON MARCH TO DOULLENS

Maj. Pringle, the second-in-command, was older than most of the other MOs, having been a senior civilian doctor who had volunteered for service when war was declared. The CO could see that he had suffered more than the younger men due to the lack of sleep and food, and the effects of a long march, and his feet were clearly giving him a lot of pain, though he tried bravely to conceal it. The Colonel therefore sent him ahead of the unit in the ambulance car to arrange billets and food for their arrival.

When they were about 3 miles from Doullens, Maj. Pringle returned with bad news. Doullens was bursting at the seams with evacuees. There was not a billet to be had and the personnel of 29CCS would have to sleep in the open outside the town. The Colonel was not prepared to accept this without a fight; his men badly needed shelter and a proper night's sleep. He returned to HQ in the ambulance car with Maj. Pringle and requested permission to divert to Gézaincourt and seek billets there.

His request was approved and the unit bypassed Doullens to the south, arriving at the village of Gézaincourt at 10.30 p.m. They had been stationed there before and had no difficulty in obtaining billets for all personnel, who enjoyed the best night's sleep they had had since the previous Wednesday.

✦✦✦

James Charles Gordon Carmichael was born on 27 August 1878 at Fort William, Calcutta, where his father, also James Charles Gordon Carmichael, a Colonel in the Indian Medical Service (IMS), was the Civil Surgeon. He came from an old family of Scottish Jacobites on his father's side, who, to their cost, had supported the House of Stewart in the monarchy struggles of the seventeenth and eighteenth centuries. His 4th, 3rd and 2nd great-grandfathers had all fought at Culloden – a major general, a colonel and a captain in the regiment their family had raised for the service of Prince Charles Edward Stewart. The family had lost all; the old man died in exile in Boulogne as a pensioner of France, and his son was incarcerated in the notorious prison ships on the Thames; but the young man was pardoned as he was only 16 years old at the time and his son took the Hanoverian King's Shilling in one of the newly raised Highland Regiments. The family had served the Crown loyally in every generation since.

His mother's family had served in India since the early days of the East India Company. His great-grandfather, a captain in the 24th Light Dragoons, had fought under Wellington in the 1st Mahratta War; his grandfather had commanded the 10th Hussars during the Mutiny and had been killed at Poona on the eve of his retirement; one uncle had been governor of Aden and of British Somaliland; and two of his cousins were serving in Indian cavalry regiments.

In 1889, at the age of 13, young James was sent home to England to attend the United Service College at Westward Ho! in Devon, a school for preparing the sons of officers for Imperial military service. Not all its alumni were army officers, though most were, and included such literary figures as Rudyard Kipling and Bruce Bairnsfather. James and his brother Donald, who was two years older than him, were at the school together and would spend their holidays with an uncle, Archibald, who was a doctor in Barrow-in-Furness in the north-west of England. Having a busy practice in the town centre, as well as being consultant surgeon at the local hospital, Uncle Archie had little spare time to entertain his nephews, to each of whom he would give a roll of tickets for the local tram company and leave the rest to their initiative and imagination.

In 1894 the two brothers went up to Edinburgh University to read medicine, graduating in 1902. The following year they were both commissioned as lieutenants on probation in the RAMC and served their early years as army doctors in India.

Then, on 27 June 1905, at a joint wedding ceremony in London, James and Donald married two sisters, Hilda and Eileen, the daughters of Lt Col James Armstrong of the IMS, who was Civil Surgeon at Cawnpore. James Armstrong was from an old Irish Ascendancy family and had graduated in medicine from Trinity College, Dublin. The two fathers had been friends and colleagues for many years.

Donald, like his father before him, was to spend almost his entire service in India. James returned to the UK in 1909 and having attended and passed the senior promotion course at the RAMC College in London, was appointed officer-in-charge of the military hospital in Manchester. Next was a posting to Malta in April 1914 as officer-in-charge of the Forrest Military Hospital. He was promoted major in October and his career was about to begin in earnest.

On the morning of Tuesday 26 March 1918, the men of 29CCS woke refreshed after their best night's sleep in almost a week. They mustered in the village square, after which, on the Colonel's orders, there was a foot inspection. The detachment was then marched to the river to wash their feet and every man was ordered to have one pair of socks washed in the village. The condition of soldiers' feet was of great importance in campaign conditions, as these medical men, who had all seen the result of neglect, knew only too well.

Their feet taken care of, the unit was marched to the site, south-west of the village where the casualty clearing stations had previously been encamped during the desperate Somme battles of 1916. 29CCS had been here at that time and the old hands, like Sgt Orr, knew the site well. There were also two other CCSs there – 3CCS, their old colleagues from Grévillers, and 56CCS, which had been the base unit at Edgehill before the attack and had managed to bring thirty-two lorry loads of hospital equipment with it from Edgehill. Under instructions from the assistant director medical services (ADMS) at Doullens, the tents and equipment were pooled between the three units and they started pitching camp. Before the tents were half up, however, the casualties started to arrive.

The three COs had a hurried conference and decided that, until they were properly established and equipped, and could recommence working as separate units, 56CCS would do all the paperwork, 3CCS would receive stretcher cases and 29CCS the walking wounded. 45CCS, one of the two hospitals which had suffered grievous casualties among its staff at Achiet-le-Grand during the early stage of the bombardment, had moved to Doullens via Aveluy and was ordered by ADMS Doullens to deliver its equipment to Gézaincourt to be divided between the three CCSs.

On Wednesday 27th, Maj. E.C. Foster RAMC and Revd W.A. Parrot joined 29CCS for temporary duty from IV Corps and, two days later, Good Friday, the Colonel was delighted to see the return of Capt. Dill and Lt Brockwell, who had accompanied the wounded on the train from Edgehill to Abbeville five days earlier. Admissions were increasing and he needed every MO he could get.

There had been steady rain throughout the week and it had been bitterly cold, which caused great difficulties with pitching tents. Towards the end of the week it became warmer, although the rain became heavier. All men who weren't engaged in admitting patients were set to trenching tents, deepening drainage ditches and spreading cinders on the floors and paths. Eventually the tents and marquees were all erected, and the wards and theatres were set up and equipped to recommence operating as an independent hospital.

The hospital site at Gézaincourt lay in a valley between two ridges of slightly higher ground, which gave some protection from winds but made drainage difficult. For security reasons, officers and men were obviously not permitted to tell families at home where they were, nor to divulge any details of current operations. On Friday 29th the Colonel wrote to his wife:

I fear that your anxiety about me will be great until you hear that I am safe. The news is good today – we are holding the Hun everywhere and our reinforcements are up … I am longing to be able to tell you all that has happened but will not be allowed to do so yet. I am in a very comfortable billet in a farmhouse ten minutes walk from my new camp. This village has never been in the war area so the houses are undamaged and all the population are still here.

The following day it rained solidly, at times very heavily, but by the evening the three COs had decided that they would be ready to start operating independently from 1 p.m. the next day.

On Easter Sunday, 31 March 1918, worshippers in churches throughout Britain, accustomed to the sombre days of Lent, arrived to find the gloomy purples of the altar frontal replaced with white and gold embroidery, which caught the sunlight flooding through chancel windows. Parish priests appeared with lighter step, their cassocks of funereal black now covered with natal white albs and chasubles of Easter white and gold. The pain and sadness of Holy Week, the agony of the crucifixion, not forgotten, but put aside for the hope and euphoric happiness of the resurrection.

At 29CCS, encamped at Gézaincourt in Picardy, Revd. Parrot got the Sergeant Major's assistance to stack some crates in a tent to form a temporary altar. Over this he spread a clean white sheet, on top of which he placed a strange, cruciform piece of twisted metal he had salvaged from a wrecked field gun on an old battleground, and which he now took everywhere with him. The white vestment he hurriedly donned over his uniform tunic was creased and in need of laundering, but to the small gathering of sick and injured men, in varying stages of pain and despair, who gathered together in the damp tent, it shone with celestial light. The simple, multi-denominational service he proceeded to conduct was as full of joy and hope as any preached in a great cathedral that morning.

Later, he performed a sadder ceremony as he led a burial party to the cemetery lying in the valley between the hospitals and laid to rest the three soldiers who had died in the CCS that day – Pte M. Kennedy (20th Durham Light Infantry); Pte R. Mansfield (110 Siege Battery, Royal Garrison Artillery); and one Australian, Pte L.G.M. Richards (42nd Battalion Australian Infantry).

The Colonel's reassurance to his wife that 'we are holding the Hun everywhere' was not entirely for her peace of mind. With a massive superiority of men and guns, the initial German attack had smashed through the British line along a 50-mile front between the Scarpe and the Oise in the first two days. At its widest, the sausage-shaped piece of land gained by the enemy on that day was about 16 miles – an extraordinary achievement in what had become a static war. The following day, 24 March, they had increased their gain by a depth of up to 10 miles in places, having taken Bapaume and Grévillers. By 26 March, the day after 29CCS had got clear of Edgehill, Albert and Edgehill had been overrun by the German advance, which then continued to sweep forward, despite desperate resistance and attempted counter-attacks, until a new frontline was more or less established by the end of the month. The territory gained by the Germans was now pear-shaped, its southern boundary formed by the Rivers Oise and Avre, then running north-east towards Lens, leaving Albert in German and Arras in British hands. It measured some 60 miles deep and 40 miles wide at its zenith.

British losses during the week had been massive: in the seven days from 22–28 March, nearly 16,000 patients had been admitted to casualty clearing stations on the Third Army front alone. Nevertheless, the British had not taken it lying down and the Germans had suffered roughly double the number of killed and wounded. It was a rule of thumb that, in this sort of engagement, on this sort of terrain, the attackers would suffer twice the defenders' losses and, although the British lines had been seriously under strength, they had been warned and were ready for the attack. However, an inevitable consequence of the speed and ferocity of the German thrust was that many British prisoners had been taken; it is estimated that some 20,000 British soldiers were captured in the first twenty-four hours alone, and that by the end of the month the Germans had taken 70,000 Allied prisoners and 1,100 guns.

By Friday 29 March, it could fairly be said that the enemy advance had been halted. There were also two other significant events on that day: firstly, at Doullens, a few miles from the Gézaincourt field hospitals, Gen. Foch was appointed as Supreme Commander of the Allied Armies in France. Whatever stimulus this may have given to fragile French morale was soon diminished with the news that, at 4.30 p.m., eighty-eight worshippers had been killed and sixty-eight injured when a German shell hit the Church of St. Gervais in the heart of Paris.

One of the benefits of the territory the enemy had gained was that Paris was now within the range of the monster 21cm gun they called Wilhelm's Gun. Paris was now in the battle zone and the Germans used this morale-destroying weapon to its maximum advantage, peppering every corner of the French capital with devastating high-explosive shells, which took three minutes and two seconds to travel the 80 miles from muzzle to target.

On Wednesday 3 April, the MOs and RAMC personnel of 29CCS were delighted to see the return of the sisters, with the arrival of six nurses from No.6 Stationary Hospital at Frèvent. They were joined two days later by two more – Sister I.M. Greaves QAIMNSR from Abbeville and Sister J. Miller QAIMNSR from No.3 Canadian Stationary Hospital, which was at the time operating from the nearby Citadelle of Doullens. Later she would have cause to be eternally thankful for this posting.

The sisters arrived just in time for a surge in admissions from 5–9 April as a result of very heavy fighting in Aveluy Wood, north of Albert, which was now occupied by the enemy, and around the village of Hébuterne. On 5 April there were 377 admissions and 345 the following day; of these, forty-one were gas cases.

On Friday 12 March, of the 239 admissions during the day, there were nine Americans from the US 11th Engineer Regiment, five sick and four wounded. Although the Americans were not yet deployed in force on the Western Front, there was one US division in the frontline and US engineers had been working for some months previously on roads, bridges and general works in preparation for the mass arrival of the 'doughboys' later in the year. It appeared that a detachment from 11th Regiment had got in the way of one of the many local German attacks along the Third Army front. Seven of the nine Americans were evacuated to base hospital the following day, but two, sadly, never made it. Pte W. Bell died of multiple gunshot wounds and Pte F. Opie, though the surgical team amputated his left arm and struggled valiantly for over an hour to stem the bleeding from several serious gunshot wounds in his left side, could not survive the trauma. They were the first two American soldiers to die in the hospital, but were certainly not the last.

The wards and treatment rooms of the hospital had a cosmopolitan air about them, containing, at any given time, a selection of British,

Australian, New Zealand, Canadian, South African and Indian soldiers, as well as members of the British West Indian and Chinese Labour Corps, French soldiers and civilians, and German prisoners of war (POWs). The medical and nursing staff, as we have already seen, also included doctors and many nursing sisters from Commonwealth countries.

It was said that in the heyday of Blackpool as a seaside resort, the locals could tell which of the northern mill towns were on their holiday week by the accents of people in the bars and the boarding houses. So it was in a casualty clearing station, with the predominant accents of the admissions giving a fair indication as to which regiments were in the line on that day. In the last week of April 1918 the wards rang with the musical cadences of Cardiff, Swansea and the Rhondda, and it was clear that the Welsh were in town.

At the beginning of April, the 38th (Welsh) Division had been moved south from its position in the line at Armentières to reinforce the badly bruised troops of the British Third Army, which, together with the Fifth Army and the French Sixth Army, had taken the brunt of the German attack in March. The division comprised three brigades consisting of one Regular and five Service battalions of the Royal Welsh Fusiliers (RWF), five Service battalions of the Welsh Regiment and two Service battalions of the South Wales Borderers. The division took up position north-west of Albert in hastily constructed and only partially finished trenches, with some trenches dating back to 1914. In the area where the frontline passed between Bouzaincourt and Aveluy the enemy held the high ground, which denied the British a view into the Ancre Valley. The 38th Division was therefore ordered to capture this ground, while the 35th Division guarded their left flank in Aveluy Wood and the Australians provided artillery support to the right.

The attack was undertaken by the six battalions of the Royal Welsh Fusiliers, who rushed the heavily defended enemy line at 7.30 p.m. on Monday 22 April. The fighting and the casualties were horrific, but the brave Welshmen succeeded in driving the enemy front back by 250yds along a 1,000yd front. This gained a position whereby the Ancre Valley could be observed and also denied the enemy their unimpeded view of the British positions.

The 13th Battalion Royal Welsh Fusiliers, on the right of the divisional line, achieved the greatest success, but also took the greatest casualties – eight officers and 263 soldiers. D Company, under Capt. C.B. Williams MC, took the final objective and held it despite violent counter-attacks at 4.40 a.m. and 7.30 a.m. the next morning. Throughout the night, the regimental stretcher bearers, assisted by soldiers of the Pioneer Battalion, evacuated 400 wounded men from the battlefield. Pte G. Stewkesbury of the Pioneers was wounded in his right eye and, though almost blind, continued evacuating the wounded until he was wounded himself a second time and lost consciousness. He was later awarded the Distinguished Conduct Medal (DCM) for his gallantry.

At the Gézaincourt field hospitals the wounded poured in throughout the night, and for several days thereafter. On 22/23 April alone, 29CCS received 244 wounded from the front and during the ensuing week buried seventeen men of the 38th (Welsh) Division in the cemetery at Gézaincourt. Of these, eleven were Royal Welsh Fusiliers. Though mostly men from the valleys, there were a few who were not Welsh, such as 20-year-old Pte George McCrovie Dickie of 13th Battalion RWF, who died from dreadful abdominal gunshot wounds on 23 April. He was from Oran Street in Maryhill, Glasgow.

And so it was in the casualty clearing stations: one week it would be Australians – big, easy-going men from Sydney and Melbourne, and from dusty settlements in the outback, who had answered the call of the motherland and were far, far from home; the next week it might be kilted Scots, 'The Ladies from Hell' as the Germans called them, from the legendary regiments of the 51st (Highland) Division. The sisters talked to them and learned a bit about every corner of the Commonwealth and of far-away places they had never heard of and could never hope to see.

The gallant Welshmen who had taken the high ground at Bouzaincourt, at such awful cost, drove off all enemy attempts to regain it and held their ground for three days and nights until they were relieved during the night of 25 April.

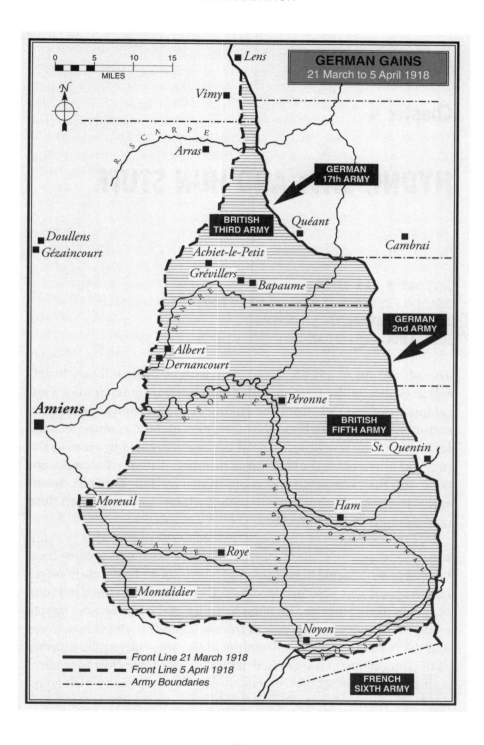

GERMAN GAINS
21 March to 5 April 1918

MILES

N

R. SCARPE

Lens

Vimy

Arras

GERMAN
17th ARMY

BRITISH
THIRD ARMY

Quéant

Cambrai

Doullens

Gézaincourt

Achiet-le-Petit

Grévillers

Bapaume

R. ANCRE

GERMAN
2nd ARMY

Albert

Dernancourt

R. SOMME

Péronne

BRITISH
FIFTH ARMY

St. Quentin

Amiens

Moreuil

Ham

R. AVRE

CANAL DU NORD

CROZAT CANAL

Roye

Montdidier

Noyon

R. OISE

Front Line 21 March 1918
Front Line 5 April 1918
Army Boundaries

FRENCH
SIXTH ARMY

Chapter 4

NYDNs, SIWs AND HUN STUFF

MONDAY 6 MAY 1918
29TH CASUALTY CLEARING STATION,
ROYAL ARMY MEDICAL CORPS,
GEZAINCOURT, FRANCE

The admissions to 29CCS, in common with all other military hospitals in France at the time, included men other than straightforward recipients of wounds from the enemy or men who were sick with common ailments such as dysentery, pneumonia, mumps or scarlet fever. As the war progressed, it became increasingly clear to the medical authorities that the large number of men who could not cope with the violence and horror of trench warfare were not, necessarily, the cowards that the Army authorities – and very often their comrades-in-arms – supposed.

During the course of the war, 306 soldiers were executed by firing squad for cowardice; many of these are now assumed to have been victims of what came to be known as 'shellshock'. In the early stages of the war, it was assumed that men showing any trace of nervous disorders were either 'trying it on' to get a ticket home or were simply cowards who were worthy only of the contempt of their fellow soldiers and the harshest treatment from the authorities. But as the number of nervous admissions increased, it gradually became clear to medical staff that not only was there a consistency of symptoms which could not be disregarded, but these were often presented in men who had already demonstrated their bravery with acts of valour which had earned them decorations and praise.

By the summer of 1917, all cases of 'shellshock' were labeled NYDN (Not Yet Diagnosed, Nervous) and were evacuated to special neurological centres where they received immediate treatment. Medical staff were instructed in the PIE principle: PROXIMITY – the patient should be treated close to the front within the sound of gunfire and battle; IMMEDIACY – nervous patients must not be kept waiting too long for treatment; and EXPECTANCY – they must understand that they would, without exception, be returned to the front after an appropriate period of rest and recuperation.

The Army authorities, naturally concerned that the acknowledgement of 'shellshock' as an illness might lead to a deluge of phoney applicants intent on 'working their ticket', introduced Army Form AF3436, which had to be completed by the patient's regimental CO before he could be officially classed as ill and treatment could proceed. This, inevitably, led to delays which rendered the 'Immediacy' element of the PIE principle largely unworkable.

By the end of the war, some 80,000 men (2% of those engaged at the front) had been diagnosed with 'shellshock'. Its severity varied from a simple nervous tic to a complete mental breakdown. Soldiers who had previously been reliable might become mute, withdrawn and completely unresponsive to outside stimulus. Others would dive under a table or cringe in a corner at the sound of any sort of commotion. Medical staff became familiar with the most common symptoms: a distant staring look in the eyes; mutism or difficulties with speech; blindness or deafness; extreme fatigue; and hysteria at the sound of gunfire.

Some soldiers would develop a neurosis related to the particular horror they might have witnessed: a man who had shot a German in the face might, himself, develop a facial tic; a man who had witnessed a friend disembowelled with a bayonet might suffer from violent stomach pains. Some would never recover.

There were then the Self-Inflicted Wounds (SIWs), men who shot themselves in the foot, or hand, to injure themselves sufficiently enough to be sent home. This was a capital offence, punishable with death by firing squad, though the maximum sentence was never enforced. Some were so desperate that they made no attempt to disguise their action; others would go to great lengths to make it appear an honourable wound received from the enemy. Shooting their foot through a sand-bag or other form of buffer to conceal any sign of powder burns was a favourite trick, but medical staff in field hospitals were under instructions to examine wounds very carefully and to interrogate patients rigorously if an SIW was suspected. If doubt still remained, bullets were sometimes sent to ordnance specialists to establish whether they were of British or German origin.

Naturally enough, SIW patients were treated with a degree of frigidity by hospital staff and other patients, particularly at busy times when they were occupying badly needed beds and demanding medical attention when others, more worthy, were waiting. Yet they, too, merited some sympathy as Colonel Carmichael wrote to his wife:

> These poor devils are placed under immediate arrest and are treated like pariah dogs by the orderlies and subjected to constant ridicule and abuse from their comrades. Certainly they have committed a despicable crime and yet one can hardly imagine the depths of despair to which a man must have descended for him to take his rifle and shatter the bones in his foot risking permanent disability and the censure and contempt of his family and friends. I cannot help but feel that he has probably served the most painful part of his sentence before he resorts to such an extreme act.

There were 3,894 convictions for Self-Inflicted Wounds during the war and all were sentenced to a term of imprisonment. But for those men who had descended to the deepest abyss of misery and desperation, there was the ultimate form of self-harm – the trench suicide. These were not uncommon, with the victim usually shooting himself in the head with his rifle by using his big toe to push the trigger. Others simply climbed out of their trench, stood exposed in no-man's-land and left the rest to enemy snipers. Often, where possible, cases of suicide were the subject of a company, or even battalion, cover-up in the interests of morale and to spare the feelings of the dead man's relatives. With the enormous volume of casualties in trench warfare, this was reasonably easy to achieve.

At 29CCS there was a fairly consistent flow of admissions through-out the month of May as the Germans launched successive thrusts along their newly acquired front and the Allies responded with some spirited counter-attacks. Around the middle of the month, there was some ferocious fighting north-west of Albert and along the Ancre Valley. The New Zealanders of the 2nd ANZAC Division were heavily involved and many of the wounded admitted to the three Gézaincourt hospitals were from this fine fighting force.

In the early hours of Sunday 12 May, all sleeping and off-duty medical staff were summoned to report to their stations to prepare for a very heavy intake of casualties from a massive German gas attack. Throughout the night and the following day the convoys of men arrived retching and gasping for breath, many crying out with the pain of their gas burns. Gas was the weapon the soldiers feared the most. At this stage of the war the Germans, having experimented with tear gases, chlorine and phosgene were using the worst gas of all, mustard gas, known to the troops as HS (Hun Stuff). Gas being heavier than air, it would roll into every trench and shell hole, reaching every remote corner and leaving an oily deposit on the ground which could remain active for weeks.

Contact with the skin caused large, intensely painful blisters filled with a yellow fluid. If more than about half of a victim's body was affected, a slow, agonising death after four to five days of suffering was almost inevitable. Thanks to the soldiers' horror of gas and their readi-ness to take the necessary precautions, most cases of gas poisoning were less severe but, nevertheless, required several weeks of treatment and convalescence. Soldiers were generally careful not to be separated from their gas masks, but if mustard gas was inhaled, it would cause bleeding and blistering of the respiratory system and lungs which, if they survived, could cause problems in later life.

During Sunday 12 May, 29CCS received 585 admissions, of which 444 had been wounded by gas. There were already 220 patients in the hospital wards. In the course of the day, two ambulance trains, Nos. 34 and 33, evacuated 182 and 114 patients respectively; five sick men were declared fit and returned to their units; eight suspected cases of dysentery were transferred to 21CCS at Aux-le-Chateau; one NYDN (one of seventeen during the month) was transferred to 45CCS, which was specialising in shellshock; two Chinese suffering from trachoma, a contagious eye disease, were transferred to the specialist eye unit in No.6 Stationary Hospital, Frèvent; and there were two deaths – Pte W. Roberts (13th Welsh Regiment) and Pte S. Smith (19th Canadians), both victims of severe gunshot wounds.

This left 496 patients, mostly gas casualties, in the hospital at night-fall. The nights were still cold in Northern France and the huge tented wards offered little protection from low temperatures. The painful blisters of the gas victims could not be bandaged or dressed, nor could the patients bear any sort of bedding or blankets on top of them. The sisters and orderlies devised all sorts of ingenious ways of construct-ing rudimentary tunnel-cages, over which blankets could be placed to keep patients warm without touching their burns; but this only provided partial relief and, with so many casualties, only the worst cases could be addressed. The cries and groans of men in acute pain resounded through the camp all night. Once again, the Colonel and his medical staff got no sleep that night as they passed from ward to ward giving whatever relief and comfort they were able to provide to the victims of the abominable 'Hun Stuff'.

Capt. J.C.G. Carmichael RAMC had arrived in Malta, together with his wife, Hilda, and his two young children, Donald and Hazel, in February 1914. After a brief spell as medical officer-in-charge with the 2nd Cameronians (Scottish Rifles) at Melleha Camp, he was appointed officer-in-charge of the Forrest Military Hospital in St Julians, a small thirty-one-bed hospital, with a twenty-bed tented overflow, which served the local British military establishment.

On 31 October 1914 he was promoted to major and, after a two-week relief posting in command of St George's General Hospital, was appointed as Commanding Officer of St. Andrew's General Hospital on 8 May 1915 – a position he held for nearly two years.

In October 1914 the Turkish Ottoman Empire had allied itself with Germany, thereby closing the Allies' only remaining viable supply route to Russia on the Eastern Front, through the Bosphorus to the Black Sea. It was therefore decided that, following a heavy naval bombardment on the Dardanelles, which failed to drive out the Turkish defenders, the Gallipoli peninsula should be secured by Allied landings. These also, despite incredible bravery and determination by British, Australian, New Zealand, French, Gurkha and Newfoundland troops, were ultimately unsuccessful. The first landings were in April 1915 and, during the nine months until the withdrawal of the Allies in January 1916, 34,000 British and Commonwealth troops were killed, of which around one third were Australians and New Zealanders. ANZAC Day on 25 April, the anniversary of the first landings, is commemorated as a national holiday in Australia and New Zealand, and is engraved deeply in the consciousness of both nations.

In addition to the large numbers killed in action at Gallipoli, there were also some 80,000 Commonwealth soldiers wounded and a far greater number who fell victim to outbreaks of dysentery and enteric fever as a result of the unsanitary conditions. The Island of Malta, conveniently situated between the battlefields and Britain, once again became 'The Nurse of the Mediterranean' and, in the spring of 1915, a frantic scramble began to commission new military hospitals to cope with the arrivals of sick and wounded. This situation became even more acute in October when another British Mediterranean front was opened in Salonika, which promised to produce as great, or even greater, volumes of sick and wounded. At the start of the war there were four British military hospitals on Malta; by mid-1916 there were twenty-seven hospitals and hospital camps on the island, with 300 MOs and almost 1,000 nurses.

St Andrew's was one of the new hospitals and Major Carmichael was given the job of converting, from scratch, what had been a huge British Army barracks into a general hospital of 1,250 beds – one of the largest on the island.

The last troops to occupy the buildings had been the 2/2 City of London Royal Fusiliers, a Territorial battalion, who handed over to the Barrack Department on 17 April 1915. The barracks were dismantled, all equipment was removed and stored, and a party of Royal Engineers moved in and whitewashed the interiors of all the buildings.

One of the major differences between military and civilian medical officers is that the former must have enormous powers of improvisation and must be ready to provide medical facilities at unbelievably short notice. In army medicine, things have to happen in conditions, and at speeds, which could not even be conceived of in civil practice. The empty shell of St Andrew's Barracks was handed over to Major Carmichael on 6 May 1915. The following day, a matron and twenty-three QAIMNS sisters arrived from England, followed two days later by fourteen MOs and eighty RAMC NCOs and men. At 3 p.m. on 12 May, the first intake of 300 wounded from Gallipoli were admitted. Remarkably, St Andrew's Military Hospital had been got 'up and running' in six days.

The fourteen MOs were all reservists, commissioned as temporary lieutenants, and comprised four surgeons, one sanitary officer, one bacteriologist and eight general physicians for ward duties.

The barracks consisted of nine identical blocks arranged in two rows ('A' to 'J', omitting 'I'), with each block having two storeys and four barrack rooms on each floor – a total of seventy-two rooms. Blocks 'A' to 'H' were designated as surgical wards and Block 'J' as medical, each ward initially containing eleven beds, though this was increased to fourteen as admissions increased. The gymnasium was converted into an additional eighty-bed ward and the old officers' mess into a sixty-bed hospital for officers.

The guard detention room was earmarked as a dispensary; the children's school was converted into an isolation hospital and two soldier-servants' rooms in the old officers' mess became X-ray and developing rooms. The butcher's shop, bakery and kitchens all retained their former roles. There was some difficulty in finding a suitable building to use as a mortuary, but a storeroom was eventually designated and equipped.

When it came to the creation of an operating theatre, which was sited in the old Maxim gun shed, Major Carmichael was very fortunate in having the advice of the eminent surgeon Sir Frederick Treeves, who was visiting Malta at the time. Sir Frederick was a pioneer of abdominal surgery and had performed an appendectomy on Edward VII, but is perhaps best remembered for his association with, and patronage of, Joseph Merrick, the famous 'Elephant Man'.

There was, naturally enough, a great shortage of equipment in the early days. The CO solicited the help of the Red Cross and the Order of St John, whose HQ was on Malta, to scour the island for beds, mattresses, pyjamas and other hospital items, and they set about the quest with missionary zeal. Eventually, 792 beds were set up, of which 200 were hospital cots, seventy were gift beds and the remainder were ordinary barrack bedsteads. Gradually these were replaced by hospital cots, and the straw mattresses by hospital hair ones, until the seventy-two wards each had fourteen proper beds, plus eighty in the gymnasium, ten in the isolation wing and sixty in the officers' hospital, providing bedded accommodation for a total of 1,158 patients.

With the versatility which only a staff trained in field conditions could show, the dispensary operated out of field medical panniers in the stripped-out old guard detention room until proper equipment arrived from England.

In a hospital of this size, a dependable laundry service was obviously of great importance. At the beginning, laundry was sent to the ASC laundry at Marsa, but the washing was not done to the required standard and often as many as 3,000 sheets were returned short. The CO therefore had the old barrack laundry resurrected and appointed civilian contractors to operate it. Consequently, there was a great improvement in the standard of laundering.

For the first two months of the hospital's operation, the majority of admissions were wounded from Gallipoli, which filled the thirty-two surgical wards; then the cases of dysentery started to arrive and later in July, cases initially admitted as enteric fever, although later, after serological and bacteriological examination, some 80 per cent of enteric admissions from Gallipoli were actually found to be paratyphoid fever.

As the year progressed, and the horrifically unsanitary conditions in Gallipoli worsened, the ratio of wounded to disease admissions was reversed and by the end of the year all the wards, except four in 'A' Block, had been changed from surgical to medical. Reports from the front told appalling stories of the conditions of squalor in which the troops were living, with rotting unburied bodies everywhere – ideal conditions for the spread of disease.

During the first nine months, 9,506 patients were admitted to St Andrew's, of which 1,636 were enterics and paratyphoids, 2,793 dysenteries, 2,620 general diseases and 2,457 battle wounded. The total mortality rate was a little over 2 per cent. In the Surgical Department

251 major and 254 minor operations had been undertaken, with 500 recoveries and five deaths.

This record from a hastily commissioned hospital, invariably overloaded and understaffed, is all the more remarkable when viewed in the context of the difficulties with which it had to contend: firstly, a high proportion of the nurses, NCOs and orderlies were untrained, partially-trained or volunteers from the New Army and St John's Ambulance Brigade, who were unfamiliar with the special requirements of battle wounded and entirely ignorant of the procedures in military hospitals. The latter could also be said of the MOs, most of whom were reservists or temporary officers. During the first nine months, sixty-one MOs were posted to the hospital, though there were rarely more than twelve at any time. Moves were so frequent that as soon as one MO had learned the ropes, he would be replaced by another inexperienced officer.

As St Andrew's reputation for excellence grew, a large proportion of serious cases from the four adjacent hospitals and one convalescent camp were transferred there for treatment in exchange for minor cases and convalescents. This deprived St Andrew's of the usual pool of willing convalescents who would normally assist the nurses and orderlies with duties around the hospital. This, in turn, put an extra strain on the hospital medical staff, who were already short-handed with an average strength of 180 compared with the 241 specified in the War Office establishment scales.

In addition to personnel difficulties, the water supply to the hospital was unpredictable in the hot weather. On one occasion a block with 112 enteric cases had no water at all for eight hours. Bath houses had to be closed during most of the hot weather with only showers available. Transport was inadequate and unpunctual, and supplies frequently failed. An interesting insight into the indulgences offered to patients on the danger list is contained in the CO's report:

On one occasion, with over 150 cases on the dangerous and serious lists, no champagne was available from the ASC but the situation was saved by the British Red Cross and Order of St. John who supplied two cases, which they purchased locally, a procedure which one would suppose could have been similarly adopted by the ASC.

Casualties from Gallipoli reached a peak in January 1916 and abated as troops were withdrawn from the peninsula. There was then a comparative lull for four to five months when the number of beds at St Andrew's was reduced from its maximum of 1,258 to 1,070. But then a serious outbreak of malaria amongst troops in Macedonia in July created a huge surge in arrivals on the island and St Andrew's expanded to 1,782 by spreading into an adjacent tented extension. The CO was promoted to local lieutenant colonel and the Malta hospitals had never been busier. In the four successive weeks of July, the hospital ships brought in 718, 1,982, 2,605 and 2,587 patients.

Admissions remained heavy for the rest of the year but, in January 1917 Germany announced that it would resume unrestricted submarine warfare. In the course of the war, ten Allied hospital ships were sunk by German submarines and a further four by mines, usually laid by submarines. With this threat to the Malta convoys, different strategies had to be introduced and admissions to the Malta hospitals declined sharply throughout the year. The busiest time of all was in October 1916 when there were 20,994 patients in military hospitals and convalescent camps on the island.

In spite of the difficulties, St Andrew's provided a superb medical service in the finest traditions of the RAMC, which spoke highly for the professionalism and dedication of the staff – particularly the small core of Regulars (about 9 per cent of total strength) who had to train their reservist and New Army colleagues as well as undertaking their own duties. But as Malta's role as 'The Nurse of the Mediterranean' declined, experienced MOs were in greater need in other theatres, and in April 1917 Lt Col Carmichael was advised that he was to be moved to the Western Front.

+ + +

After the casualties of the heavy gas attacks of 12 May 1918 had been evacuated to base hospitals up the line, admissions to 29CCS at Gézaincourt settled down to a steady flow of, on average, 118 a day, of which about one third were wounded and two thirds sick.

From 15 May–1 June, however, the Germans undertook a bombing campaign directed at Allied hospitals, during which 248 were killed and 693 wounded. Around midnight on 27/28 May, German aircraft bombed No.3 Canadian Stationary Hospital, which was operating from a building within the ancient Citadelle at Doullens. One bomb struck the central staircase in the main building to the side of the wards and destroyed the officers' ward and the operating theatre below it, which was in use at the time. Three MOs, three sisters, the whole of the theatre staff and ten officers from the ward above were buried in the wreckage. Out of forty-two staff at the hospital, thirteen were killed in this attack.

Captain E.E. Meek of the Canadian Medical Services, Sisters D.M. Baldwin, E.L. Pringle and A. McPherson, together with nine Canadian orderlies from the hospital were buried the following day in the cemetery at Gézaincourt.

Damage to the hospital was so extensive, and losses of personnel so great, that the authorities decided to reduce it to a skeleton strength while emergency repairs were undertaken. Consequently, on 30 May, Capt. N.S. Richardson RAMC and Capt. C. Kerby RAMC with thirty-three orderlies, all from No.3 Canadian Stationary Hospital, reported for temporary duty at 29CCS.

Sister J. Miller, a senior theatre sister who had been transferred to 29CCS from No.3 Canadian Stationary Hospital the previous month, was shocked, but eternally thankful, when she learned of the fate of her erstwhile colleagues, which she so easily might have shared.

017 St Andrew's Hospital, Malta, 1917

018 & 019 The CO is front row centre between the two matrons in both groups.

020 British, French and German wounded receive treatment at 29 Casualty Clearing Station, Gézaincourt, 27 April 1918. © Imperial War Museum (Q8734)

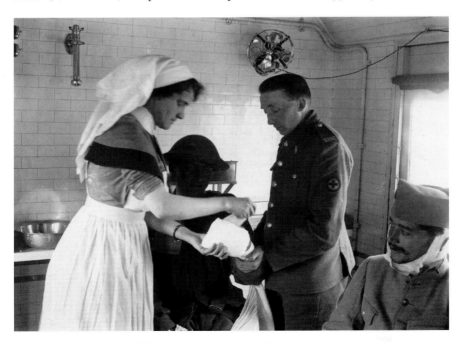

021 A Sister and an RAMC Orderly dress a patient's wounds on board an Ambulance Train at Gézaincourt. © Imperial War Museum (Q8737)

022 A Sister attends to patients aboard Ambulance Train No.29 at Gézaincourt on 27 April 1918. The train left the following day with 128 patients. (The French "Poilu" in the top bunk was obviously enjoying the publicity as he also appears in both pictures opposite which were all taken during the same official photography shoot.) © Imperial War Museum (Q8736)

023 Awaiting arrival of the patients. © Imperial War Museum (Q8738)

us - firing over us. more of our heavies alongside and an enormous gun on two trucks on the railway just on the other side of us. all blazing away at the same time - when night came I had wired for more & more cars to take away the wounded - & they came in bigger numbers so that we were keeping pace - as soon as it was dark Hun planes came over us dropping bombs all around us - & of course the gun fire never ceased. There were many narrow escapes. That night again no one went to bed - & at 2 A.M. I was told to hand over the 2nd C.C.S. to a Field Ambulance. & clear out my personnel by good train - By this time there were only 6 wounded left in Hospital - as I had deflected the ambulance cars for some hours. I got all my officers & men into the trucks - & then found that the huge gun on the railway had blocked our way. Eventually the train went off. I stayed behind with the O's mr to make sure that there were no stragglers - & that everything had been saved - then about 3. A.M. he & I went off by car to a place about 10 miles back. where I was to meet the train with my detachment - & where the train with all my tents & equipment had been sent the day before. I did not arrive till 6 A.M. as I had to go a long way out of my way to report events at Head Qrs. On arrival I was so sleepy that I lay down in a filthy

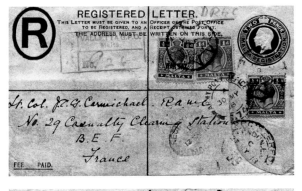

024
Communications
to and from the
frontline.

ACTIVE SERVICE

A.F.W. 9072.
W299/M1930 4/17.
M. & S. LTD.

This envelope must not be used for coin or valuables. It cannot be accepted for registration.

NOTE:—

Correspondence in this envelope need not be censored Regimentally. The contents are liable to examination at the Base.

The following Certificate must be signed by the writer:—

I certify on my honour that the contents of this envelope refer to nothing but private and family matters.

Signature
Name only } *J.C.J. Carmichael*

[Several letters may be forwarded in this Cover, but these must all be from the same writer. The Cover should then be given in such case to the Base Censor.]

Address :—

Mrs H. S. Carmichael
No 200 Strada It Torri
Sliema
Malta .

A.F.A. 2042.
114/Gen.No./5248.

FIELD SERVICE POST CARD

The address only to be written on this side. If anything else is added the post card will be destroyed.

Mrs H.S. Carmichael
No 200 Strada It Torri
Sliema
Malta

025 The Field Service Post Card on which only the minimum amount of news was allowed to be conveyed to worried relatives at home.

NOTHING is to be written on this side except the date and signature of the sender. Sentences not required may be erased. If anything else is added the post card will be destroyed.

[Postage must be prepaid on any letter or post card addressed to the sender of this card.]

I am quite well.

~~I have been admitted into hospital~~
{ ~~sick~~ ~~and am going on well.~~
~~wounded~~ ~~and hope to be discharged soon.~~ }

I am being sent down to the base.

~~I have received your~~ { letter dated _____
telegram .. _____
parcel ,, _____ }

Letter follows at first opportunity.

~~I have received no letter from you~~
{ ~~lately~~
~~for a long time.~~ }

Signature only } *J.C.J. Carmichael.*

Date _____

Wt. W1546. R1618.18539. 8000m. 6-17. C. & Co., Grange Mills, S.W.

Picked in the trenches before Arras, + on their old battle-fields - also in the village of Fampoux.

026 Pressed wild flowers picked on the battlefield and enclosed with a letter.

027 Lieutenant Colonel James Allman Armstrong IMS Civil Surgeon Cawnpore. (Father-in-Law of JCGC)

028 Colonel James Charles Gordon Carmichael IMS Civil Surgeon Fort William, Calcutta. (Father of JCGC)

029 Hilda Sade Carmichael (née Armstrong). (Wife of JCGC)

030 Colonel Donald Roy Gordon Carmichael. (Son of JCGC)

031 James Charles Gordon Carmichael on commissioning as a Lieutenant RAMC in 1902.

032 A kilted Highland soldier outside the Collecting Post for Walking Cases at 69 Field Ambulance amidst the desolation of the Western Front. © Wellcome Library, London

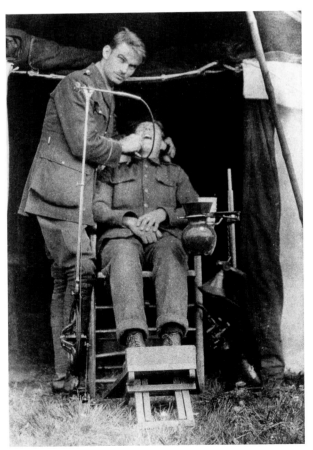

033 A Dental Officer attached to a Casualty Clearing Station. There was an acute shortage of dentists at the beginning of the war until the C-in-C instituted a recruiting drive following severe toothache for which he had difficulty in obtaining treatment. © Wellcome Library, London

Chapter 5

THE YANKS ARE COMING!

3 JUNE 1918
29TH CASUALTY CLEARING STATION,
ROYAL ARMY MEDICAL CORPS,
GEZAINCOURT, FRANCE

It did not take the Royal Engineers long to complete emergency repairs on the Canadian hospital at Doullens and make it fit to resume admissions. Three days later, on Monday 3 June, the two MOs and twenty-eight of the thirty-three orderlies on temporary loan to 29CCS returned to their stations in the Citadelle.

June heralded a period of relative stability at Gézaincourt and, during June, July and the first three weeks of August, with no major conflagrations to invoke emergency admission or evacuation procedures, the hospitals settled down to the regular and ordered routine of British military field hospitals. Spirits were generally higher with the long days of summer, with convalescent patients able to sit outside their tents and enjoy the fresh air and sunshine. Lighter workloads gave the staff a temporary respite from the endless routine of work and sleep with no leisure time between the two, and the nurses had more frequent opportunities to write to their families at home and to chat to, and spend more time with, patients in the wards, which was always good for morale.

Regular drills and inspections, necessarily discarded during periods of intense pressure, were reintroduced: the acting Sergeant Major conducted night duties drill at 7.15 a.m. and day duties at 2 p.m. each day; Maj. Grant, the second-in-command, held an officers' drill at 9 a.m. daily; and the CO had a night duties inspection at 6.45 p.m. and a day duties inspection, fifteen minutes later, at 7 p.m.

Following instruction and practice in gas mask drill by the CO and Cpl Falkner, the gas NCO, the newly arrived Regimental Sergeant Major (RSM) H. Charlesworth put the nursing sisters through their paces with a competition between day and night sisters for the best time for gas alert 'with masks at the ready'. The day sisters won with a best time of six seconds, three seconds faster than the night sisters at nine seconds.

On 19 June the first Russians appeared in the hospital with the admission of eleven sick soldiers. They seemed like broken men to the staff, having been involved in the brutal fighting on the Eastern Front and with their homeland now in political and social turmoil, and having no idea of whether their families at home were alive or dead. Communication was difficult, but one sister who spoke a little Russian was able to draw out of them that many had heard nothing from, or of, their families for nearly two years.

Lt Col Carmichael, for the first time in three months, was able to resume his evening walk, as he told his wife in a letter on 26 June. He was not, of course, allowed to tell her where he was in a letter, but had asked one of his officers who had been posted to Malta to tell her 'Doullens', and to show her where it was on a map, so he could give her an indication as to where he was by reference to 'the place Campbell told you':

I am two and a half miles from the place that Campbell told you in a valley between two small hills. This country is extremely pretty for it is mostly hills covered with woods in which there is a profusion of wild flowers. Sometimes when I go for a walk in the woods in the evening I bring back armfuls of honeysuckle and other wild flowers for the wards. The countryside is green and unscarred by ruined buildings and shell craters, quite unlike the land further forward which is simply a great expanse of devastation with trees, hedges, fields and houses unrecognisable as what they once were. Here, the farmhouses remain intact with their original inhabitants living and working the fields around them. If it wasn't for the constant rumble of gunfire and the noise of the trains and ambulances arriving and departing all the time with patients, we could be in the depths of the countryside in a land at peace. How I would love to have you and the children here – what grand picnics we could have.

Although the first American troops had been in France since June 1917, there had been transportation problems and the build-up had been slow. The first major participation of the United States in the war had been in late October 1917, and one US division had played an active part in the defensive actions of March/April 1918, with three more ready in reserve. However, by May 1918 there were one million American troops in France, with another 500,000 expected by the end of August. The 'Yanks' were ready for serious action as the chorus of a song popular in America at the time suggested:

Over there, over there,
Send the word, send the word, over there,
That the Yanks are coming,
The Yanks are coming,
The drums rum-tumming everywhere.
So prepare, say a prayer,
Send the word, send the word to beware,
We'll be over, we're coming over,
And we won't come back 'til it's over, over there.

Americans were no longer a novelty to the staff at 29CCS; as already mentioned, United States Army engineers had been working on preparations for the mass arrivals of the infantry for some time. Several had been admitted as patients and, as already recorded, two US Army engineers had sadly died of wounds in the hospital during April.

There were also a large number of American volunteer MOs supporting the hard-pressed British medical services in France and there had hardly been a period during 1918 when at least one American MO was not working in the hospital. They were extremely competent professionally, deeply committed to the cause they had volunteered to assist and a great asset to the many establishments in which they served. There was also an American AT in service, No.61 USAT, which was making regular trips between the Gézaincourt and base hospitals.

On 26 June the CO wrote to his wife:

> We were all very bucked at the war news this morning. If the Austrians collapse the Hun will really be in difficulties. Then there seems to be a great chance that both Japan and China will send troops to Siberia and our American friends are arriving in great numbers, determined to give Fritz a bloody nose, so I am still hopeful that we may be together again before the end of the year.

By August 1918 there were one and a half million US troops in France and there was talk, if the war had not already been won, of a one hundred-division US attack in 1919.

Long before America had declared war on Germany, the Allies' desperate need of additional medical personnel and facilities in France had been well publicized, and many Americans had come forward as volunteers to offer their services. The medical faculties of several US universities set about raising staff and equipment to provide individual field hospitals.

One such was the Northwestern University in Chicago where Dr Frederick A. Besley, a surgeon at the school of medicine, in conjunction with the American Red Cross, raised what was initially known as the Northwestern University Base Hospital (Chicago Unit) and was officially called No.12 US Army Base Hospital, with Dr Besley as its first director and chief of surgical services. The unit consisted of twenty-three doctors, two dentists, sixty-five nurses and 150 men, and was equipped, initially, for 500 patients. The doctors came mainly from Northwestern University and the nurses were recruited from various Chicago training establishments. Three quarters of the men engaged as orderlies, stretcher bearers, drivers, etc., were students at the university.

The unit sailed from New York on 19 May 1917 on board the USS *Mongolia*, a former immigrant ship acquired by the US government as a troop transport. It was one of five ships that sailed during the month with medical personnel for France. The ship was fitted with three 6in deck guns, manned by gunners of the US Navy, and during firing practice on the first day of the voyage a percussion cap ricocheted off a stanchion, injuring several bystanders and killing two nurses, Edith Ayers and Helen Wood. They were two of the earliest US medical casualties of the war.

On 2 June the USS *Mongolia* arrived at Falmouth in Cornwall where it was met by King George V and Queen Mary. The King addressed the Northwestern unit, thanking the volunteers personally and expressing the nation's deep gratitude for their timely aid. From Falmouth they sailed to Boulogne where they landed on 11 June, the second US hospital unit to arrive in France.

After spending their first night at Boulogne, they were taken in charabancs (motor coaches) for 16 miles down the coast to Camiers, the site of the British No.18 General Hospital, which would become No.12 US Base Hospital when they had taken it over.

Camiers Camp was part of the vast British military base depot complex at Etaples (known to the troops as 'Eat Apples'). It contained enormous ordnance and equipment depots, which supplied much of the frontline units. In 1917 there were some 100,000 troops camped among the dunes around Etaples and Camiers, and No.18 General Hospital was one of seventeen military and Red Cross hospitals within the complex.

When the Americans arrived, the British medical staff had already left the hospital and a skeleton British staff consisting of the registrar, the matron, the assistant matron, the senior home sister and night sister remained for a period to assist the incoming staff with settling in and becoming acquainted with the workings of a military hospital. The Americans were met and welcomed by the British matron, Miss Williams, the assistant matron, Miss Bennet and the registrar, who would also become liaison officer to the unit, Maj. J.C.G. Carmichael RAMC. The matron-in-chief of the BEF visited the hospital in the afternoon of 19 June and recorded in her diary that the American matron, Miss Urch, and her assistant were both delighted with the hospital and with the arrangements made for their reception and comfort.

When he had been posted from Malta on 20 April 1917, Lt Col Carmichael had lost his temporary rank and reverted to his substantive rank of major. He arrived in Camiers on 29 April to take up his appointment as registrar of No.18 General Hospital.

Immediately on his arrival he applied to the DMS for a more active appointment commanding a field ambulance or casualty clearing station. Though he had the qualifications, experience and recommendations, there was a great shortage of Regular MOs, and DMS insisted that the position of liaison officer to the newly arrived American allies should be an experienced Regular officer. Moreover, as the appointment was for a major, he had no chance of regaining his temporary rank of lieutenant colonel as long as he remained in this post.

In June, while awaiting arrival of the American unit, the weather in France was oppressively hot, with temperatures well in excess of 80°F. Having only Viyella shirts and European standard issue heavy serge uniforms, Maj. Carmichael was very uncomfortable:

> But I have no business to complain when I remember that you and the children must be suffering far greater heat and discomfort in Malta. If your sandfly nets have become worn, dear, you must buy new ones; the comparatively small expenditure is not to be considered as you are all particularly susceptible to insect bites and are all very bad about scratching! ... This afternoon James and I got caught in very heavy rain while out for a walk but we found shelter in a store tent. Then all this evening we have had violent thunderstorms with deluges of tropical rain like the monsoon in India. The lightning is extraordinary – sheet and forked together. How I pity the poor fellows in the trenches who are having to suffer these extremes of weather in addition to their normal perils.... We expect the Americans here early next week.

When the Americans duly arrived, it was found that the unit, in common with the other American medical units arriving in France, was below the requirements of the British War Establishment, having only sixty-four nurses as opposed to seventy-five per 1,040 beds. Twenty-five British Voluntary Aid Detachment (VAD) members were drafted in to bring the hospital up to strength until reinforcements of US Army nurses arrived from America.

Maj. Carmichael soon began to recognise the differences between British and American procedures. Two of the most fundamental were the use of anaesthetists and dieticians: American hospitals, he learned, had a long tradition of nursing sisters acting as anaesthetists – an extremely valuable accomplishment with the growing shortage of MOs in the forward areas. In due course, all six American hospitals therefore offered training facilities in anaesthesia for nurses, who then finished their course with a one-month attachment to a casualty clearing station. Later in the war, sisters of several of the Allied nursing services did sterling work as anaesthetists in the surgical teams of field hospitals at the front.

Dieticians were also used to an extent not normally found in British hospitals. Most American units had one civilian dietician and the Chicago unit had two. These dieticians were responsible for supervision of the general diet in the hospital and all matters pertaining to the preparation and serving of food. They were also responsible for special diets which they decided upon in conjunction with the sister-in-charge for patients with conditions demanding them – gastritis, nephritis, post-operative patients, etc. These meals were prepared in a special diet kitchen using supplies obtained partly from the QM and partly from the American Red Cross.

The work of the American dieticians proved of great interest to the British medical authorities. The advice of the American chief nurses was sought in the training of dieticians and a British sister was seconded to an American unit for several weeks to observe their practices and obtain experience of their duties.

On 3 July, Maj. Carmichael wrote to his wife before 7 a.m. explaining that he had been called up for a convoy arriving at 4.45 a.m. and expressing the hope that the two American MOs whom he was training in convoy work would soon be able to manage on their own. He had had very few unbroken nights' sleep since arriving in France.

He also told her that they were expecting an imminent visit from the Queen, possibly with the King:

> It will be interesting to see them again. It is now over eleven years since we were presented to them in Madras. I don't suppose I shall have an opportunity of speaking to them for I suspect they will be surrounded by the Headquarters brass hats and will only have the senior Yanks introduced to them.

He was very impressed with the American personnel:

> Not only are they extremely competent but they are totally dedicated to the service of our soldiers. There is a very relaxed and happy atmosphere in the wards; the patients tease the nurses about their funny accents and the nurses give back as good as they get yet nobody oversteps the bounds of mutual respect. The MOs are extremely friendly and kind. Just now, first one of their old Majors gave me an orange and two minutes later another presented me with four. My protests were of no avail. One never sees fruit here; the fruit hawkers will not come out as far as this whereas five miles down the road there are hundreds of them but I seldom have a chance to leave the hospital for long enough to avail myself of their services.

When he needed the odd bit of mending or a button sewn on, he would take it to the old assistant matron:

> One thinks when one first meets her that she is wearing some grotesque mask. But her harrowing ugliness is totally transcended by her generous spirit and compassionate nature. She is a truly remarkable woman who is always ready to help those who need it. She took me to tea with the Matron of a neighbouring hospital yesterday.... There is to be a boxing match this evening between our fellows and the Americans. There is much excitement about it and there is a good deal of betting taking place which we are not supposed to know about! ... The war news is excellent. The Russians have started fighting again and have taken 10,000 prisoners. I was talking to a Staff Officer from General Headquarters today and he said he would take on any bet that the war would be over by Christmas.

As the Americans became more and more familiar with hospital routines, Maj. Carmichael again applied for command of a forward hospital and was again turned down, as a Regular RAMC major was apparently essential in the position he held and there was no suitable officer in France to replace him. When he could leave the pressure of the hospital routine for an hour or two, his favourite relaxation was to walk with the padre, or one of the American MOs, to a nearby pine wood with several large poplars, under one of which they would sit for a smoke amid a carpet of wild pansies before returning. On 12 July, together with other medical staff, he attended gas instruction at a nearby training establishment:

> We were put into a long, underground dugout like a narrow tunnel and then a huge cylinder of gas was turned towards us and the valve opened. Volumes of greenish yellow gas rolled all over us but, of course, one suffered no ill effects as we had our gas masks on. All my buttons which were beautifully shiny immediately turned black. Likewise the gold pin in my collar. Of course, we had been warned that this would happen and had removed our belts and wrist watches. It was quite an interesting experience but seems rather a waste for those unfortunates, like myself, who seem destined to remain at the base.

But his patience was to be rewarded and before the end of the month he heard, semi-officially, that his appointment to command a field ambulance would come through as soon as he could be relieved by a trustworthy Regular major. This might take up to a month, or slightly more, he was told, and would mean that he would, almost immediately, regain his rank of temporary lieutenant colonel. In the first week of August he received notification that his move was imminent. On the 15th he was dined out by the Americans:

> ... and what a magnificent send off they gave me! Colonel Collins the C.O. made a most flattering speech which met with rapturous applause. What I thought was so nice was to conclude he said: 'Gentlemen, I ask you to rise to drink the health of Major C., Mrs. C. and their children; I particularly wish to associate his family in our toast.' My reply went off much better than I had expected for it produced roars of laughter and a thunderous ovation at the end. Old Wood, who was one of the guests, said to me afterwards: 'By Jove Major, you made a ripping speech!' I wrote it out in advance and then learned it by heart so I did not have to keep looking at my notes. I would send you a copy but I'm afraid the references would mean little to you as you do not know the peculiarities of the officers concerned. I have been bombarded with good wishes and little presents from these kind, kind people, several of whom have pressed me to come and stay with them if I should ever have cause to visit the Chicago area after the war. Our Nation owes these doctors,

nurses and orderlies a deep debt of gratitude. They have sacrificed much in terms of their career progression and prospects to help us in our hour of need. I hope, when it is all over, we will never forget this generosity and the deep bond of friendship it implies. Tonight I am being dined out by a neighbouring hospital.

On 25 August 1917, Maj. Carmichael bade farewell to his American friends at Camiers and joined No.11 Field Ambulance, 'somewhere in France', to commence his induction in frontline medicine.

Throughout July 1918 and the first three weeks of August, life was comparatively quiet in 29CCS at Gézaincourt. During the whole month of July there were only 2,169 admissions – 1,638 sick and 531 wounded, including 261 gas cases. There were thirty-five deaths.

On a few days there were no admissions at all. The Padre, Revd R. Holme, used the opportunity to take some leave, returning to the unit on 23 July. On 31 July the CO said a reluctant farewell to his second-in-command, Maj. M.F. Grant RAMC, who was posted to take command of 150 Royal Navy (RN) Field Ambulance. The new Sergeant Major, RSM Charlesworth, used the period of comparative calm to hone his men and the hospital procedures to peacetime levels of efficiency; no excuses were given or taken for unpolished buttons or unshaven faces when the night duty and day duty, each of approximately twenty NCOs and men, were inspected daily.

Although things were quiet at Gézaincourt, the great lion which was the Allied armies in France was starting to stir and a sense of anticipation pervaded the hospital. News came in daily of the start of serious fighting at various points along the line. On 15 July the Germans attacked along a 50-mile front around Rheims in a final lunge towards Paris. East of Rheims the line held, but to the west the enemy broke through and formed a new salient bubble around Chateau-Thierry. The following day, the day on which the Russian Tsar and his family were murdered by the Bolsheviks, French and American armies counter-attacked, pricking the bubble and driving the intruders steadily back to the Chemin-des-Dames. The tide was beginning to turn.

Chapter 6

PAYBACK TIME!

On Tuesday 20 August 1918, there were two wounded admissions to 29CCS; the following day there were 782, plus seventy-seven wounded German POWs. The Battle of Bapaume, the second phase in the long-awaited Allied offensive, had begun. IV and VI Corps of the British Third Army, with the US II Corps attached, had smashed into the German line along a 9-mile front north of the Ancre from Hamel to Moyenneville. By nightfall they had advanced to the Albert–Arras railway.

Although things had been quiet at the Gézaincourt hospitals during the first three weeks of August, the great Allied offensive had actually started two weeks earlier when, on Thursday 8 August, the British Fourth Army and the French First Army, following a heavy artillery bombardment, had broken through the German lines to the south. By nightfall on the first day they had advanced the line by about 6 miles, and by the following Tuesday the extreme right of the British line, where it joined the French sector, had been pushed up by some 15 miles to the west of Chaulnes. Fourteen infantry divisions, including the US 33rd Division, three cavalry divisions and 400 tanks had taken part. The Germans had received a bloody nose, but there was worse to follow.

The casualty clearing stations in the Fourth Army area had dealt with the wounded from this early part of the offensive, but on 21 August the Third Army attack was the prelude to a far heavier and more widespread operation. On the 22nd, III Corps recaptured the town of Albert, then, on the next day, the full fury of the Allied retaliation was hurled against the heavily fortified German positions along a 30-mile front from the junction with the French in the south to Mercatel in the First Army area to the north.

For the next eight days the old battlefields of the Somme, the scenes of the terrible carnage of 1916, were fought over once again, but this time with very real gains by the Allies. On 29 August the British recaptured Bapaume and at the end of this phase of the offensive, on the night of 31 August, the Australian Corps crossed the Somme and broke the German lines at Mont St Quentin, overlooking Peronne. Gen. Rawlinson, commander of the Fourth Army, was to describe the Australian advance from 31 August to 4 September as 'the greatest military achievement of the war'. Twenty-three Allied divisions had taken part in the Battle of Bapaume and had captured 34,000 prisoners and 270 guns.

The cost in casualties was necessarily high. In the fighting from 21–24 August, the twelve casualty clearing stations in the Third Army sector admitted 13,275 Allied and 1,018 German wounded. The bulk of these were directed to the three hospitals at Gézaincourt and the two at Frévent. A surgical team from 47CCS at Fillièvres was sent to establish an advanced operating centre at Le Bac-de-Sud on the First Army boundary. In the subsequent fighting, from 25 August to the end of the month, a further 16,166 Allied and 968 German casualties were admitted to the Third Army CCSs.

During this period the three hospitals at Gézaincourt worked around the clock to keep pace with the continuous arrival of wounded soldiers, forwarding them on as expeditiously as the arrival of ambulance trains would allow to No.6 Stationary Hospital at Fillièvres. From 21–31 August 29CCS admitted 3,649 Allied and 308 German wounded. As soon as one loaded ambulance train pulled out from the Gézaincourt siding, another empty one pulled in and the loading of wounded began again. But despite this continuous shuttle, the trains could not keep up and large numbers of wounded remained each night in the hospital ward tents, which were sometimes filled to overflowing with stretchers lying in rows in other areas. On the night of the 21st there were 620 patients remaining at 29CCS and, in the nights that followed, there were seldom less than 300–400.

Fortunately, HQ DMS had been warned in advance of the forthcoming attack and had made some preparations for the deluge: on 20 August an RAMC surgical team consisting of two MOs, one sister and three orderlies had reported for duty at 29CCS, and the following day, in which over 900 patients were admitted, there was a large augmentation of medical staff with the arrival, at different times throughout the day, of two American and four Canadian MOs, four sisters, three staff nurses, and nineteen RAMC and five Canadian Army Medical Corps (CAMC) orderlies. Every one of them was fully employed around the clock. An extra chaplain, Revd A.C. Williman, also reported for temporary duty and his services were also very much in demand. In the ten days of the battle, there were 154 deaths in the hospital, a higher death rate than ever before, even at the height of the German March offensive. Every day the chaplains conducted their dolorous ceremonies in the little burial ground in the valley. The cost of advance, it seemed, was even greater than the cost of retreat.

When Maj. Carmichael left his post as registrar and liaison officer to No.12 US Base Hospital, he was anxious to obtain command of a field ambulance as soon as possible. However, before he could be considered for such, it was necessary for him to obtain some experience in frontline medicine and to see at firsthand the work done by the RAPs in the trenches and the procedures in the advanced dressing stations (ADS), main dressing stations (MDS), field ambulances and casualty clearing stations. Therefore, on 27 August 1917 he reported for temporary duty with No.11 Field Ambulance somewhere in the 4th Division area. He later wrote to his wife:

I have had a most interesting time since last I wrote to you. I have been up to the front line to see and follow the whole evacuation chain for our wounded from the Regimental Aid Posts in the foremost trenches, through the various dressing stations until they reach a Field Ambulance or Casualty Clearing Station. It is a wonderful bit of planning and organisation which gives these poor devils the best possible chance of recovery from some of the terrible wounds they receive.

On Monday (this is Thursday) I went up after breakfast to an Advance Dressing Station which was situated about a mile in front of our artillery positions and about a mile behind the front line trenches. Shells, both from our own guns behind and the German guns ahead, were constantly passing over our heads. There was a deep cellar below the Station into which all personnel bolt when the shells come too close. This happens very infrequently as the Bosche does not waste his ammunition.

In the afternoon I went for a mile up a communication trench and then down a 30-foot pit in which a large periscope was mounted – just like the one we saw in that submarine we went over. Through this one can examine no-man's land and the surrounding country minutely and can observe what the enemy are up to in and behind their trenches. From what I could see, their trenches seem better and more permanently built than our own.

Later I was taken to a ruined village which the Bosche rarely shells now. It is now no more than a mass of rubble with odd little bits of wall still standing here and there. It is so sad to think that this was once a village with children playing, church bells ringing and women doing their shopping. What a lot these poor people have suffered. There is nothing of their old way of life still recognisable. I suppose most of them are living somewhere with relatives or friends in a safer part of France.

Outside the village I had the chance to examine a derelict tank. It was the first time I had seen one close to. They are amazing things – massive, heavily armoured and distinctly sinister. I suspect that they will become the battlefield weapons of the future but the engineers will have to do something about improving their mobility as one sees many of them bogged down and abandoned in the mud.

From a deep cutting outside this village I watched a fight between a British and German aeroplane and our planes being shelled by anti-aircraft guns. Further down the road I stumbled and twisted my ankle – I had tripped over the severed head of a dead German.

After supper when it was quite dark, I walked for about two miles along a road which can not be used in day time as it is in full view of the Germans and here I hunted about in old German ammunition dumps and found a big, empty shell case which I took back with me. I will have it cut down, polished and made into an ashtray. That night I slept on the ground in the deep cellar.

After breakfast the next day, I went by motor car to another Advanced Dressing Station. On the way we came under shell fire at a point where the road passed close to our own artillery positions. We had to leave the car and shelter behind a ruined wall until the shelling had eased. I had lunch at this Advanced Dressing Station and then walked over the open ground behind our lines to see some relay posts and ended in a communication trench where there was an Aid Post. From here I returned to the ADS and shortly after my arrival there was a tremendous explosion. The window frames which were covered with muslin were blown in and smoke, dust and earth flew into the shelter. There were about five officers in the room and all dived for their tin hats and gas masks and made a rush for the cellar. I learned later that it was not a shell but a nearby ammunition dump blowing up. I could not return by road as I had intended as the Germans were now shelling it so I got a ride on a canal barge back to 11th Field Ambulance who were due to move the next day.

The next day the field ambulance moved to a new position about 10 miles to the rear. The march took four hours, but Carmichael was fortunate in having the use of a horse. In the evening, he and the CO rode out to examine the surrounding countryside, noting all the special features and identifying them on their service maps; they never knew when they might have to move in a hurry.

His frontline induction complete, Maj. Carmichael applied for an interview with DMS for consideration for command of a field ambulance. In the meantime, he was posted for temporary duty to 5CCS, which was encamped at Tincourt, near Péronne, in the Fourth Army area. He remained here from 16 September until 28 October 1917, during which time he heard that his interview had been successful and he was to take command of 29CCS on 29 October. While writing to his wife with the good news, he was anxious to reassure her that he was in little danger:

You need have no anxiety for me. Service in a Casualty Clearing Station is almost as safe as in a Base Hospital on the coast. The casualties among MOs that you hear about are nearly always very junior officers serving in the Regimental Aid Posts in the front line. Theirs is indeed a hazardous employment and one hears of many instances of great gallantry among these young chaps many of whom are only recently out of medical school.

He left 5CCS on 28 October 1917 and made his way north to Grévillers, near Bapaume, in the Third Army area. The following day he took over command of 29CCS from Lt Col J.H. Brunskill RAMC who, only three days earlier, had received notice of a posting to Mesopotamia. John Handfield Brunskill was an Irishman who had completed his medical training at Trinity College, Dublin and had played cricket for Dublin. He had scored 25 and 58 when they beat the Marylebone Cricket Club during their 1895 tour. Col Brunskill had been commanding 29CCS at Gézaincourt in November 1916 when a train full of men going on leave had caught fire in the station. Fourteen men had been burned to death and staff from the CCS, including Sgt John Orr, had shown great courage and presence of mind in attempting to rescue the trapped occupants. Col Brunskill had been a popular and well-respected CO and would clearly be a hard act to follow.

The hospital site at Grévillers was about a ¼ mile outside what had once been a typical Picardy village, with a church and central square, a few shops and clusters of little houses built with the distinctive local red brick. In 1918 it was mainly heaps of rubble with the few, windowless buildings left standing being used by the Army for temporary billets and stores. There were casualty clearing stations on both sides of the road, opposite each other, sharing the same railway siding for evacuating patients and the same burial ground for those who did not make it.

A casualty clearing station was a very substantial organisation: theoretically, there was one CCS per division, each catering for an in-patient strength of 200. In practice, on the busier fronts in times of heavy activity, the numbers swelled to three or four times the establishment and there were seldom periods when 29CCS had fewer than twice the laid-down number of patients. For an in-patient strength of 400, a CCS would typically be staffed by around 200 officers and men with three attached chaplains. When operating in the field, it was a huge tented encampment occupying a site of about ½ sq mile, consisting of around sixty marquees and forty bell tents. The War Establishment stated that a 200-bed CCS would require seventeen horse-drawn General Service Wagons or eight 3-ton motor lorries to move. In practice, as the war progressed, the greatly expanded CCSs required between fifty and a hundred lorries. When moving by rail, as frequently happened, a CCS would often require a whole goods train to accommodate its stores, tents and equipment.

In addition to its medical staff, the CCS would have attachments of ASC drivers, Royal Engineers to provide and maintain the water supply, and Pioneers to dig latrines and the drainage ditches which surrounded the encampment, though much of the manual labour in field hospitals was undertaken by the ever-willing VD convalescents of which there was always an abundance.

There had been no 'handover period' when Maj. Carmichael took command of 29CCS on 29 October 1917; he shook hands with Col Brunskill, who wished him well and left the hospital en route to England for two weeks leave before taking up his posting in Mesopotamia. Within minutes, the new CO was touring the wards in the company of his second-in-command and sergeant major.

On Sunday 1 September 1918, Capt. F.R. Wilson RAMC, a dental surgeon, joined 29CCS for temporary duty. Dentistry in the Army had been a pretty crude business prior to 1901, confined almost exclusively to the extraction of rotten teeth by regimental surgeons with no form of anaesthesia. Prior to this, it was often undertaken by the regimental farrier or by an NCO who was handy with the pliers. During the Second Boer War, a heavy demand for dentistry resulted in the formation of a Dental Service Branch within the RAMC in 1901 but, with the massive enlistment during the First World War, the branch was completely overwhelmed and extraction duties had reverted, in the main, to regimental MOs.

Then, one day, FM Earl Haig, the commander-in-chief, was struck with the misery of toothache and was told it might be weeks before an Army dentist could attend him. He was not prepared to wait and sent for a French dentist from Paris to extract his tooth but, within weeks, ever mindful of the welfare of his men, he had instigated a huge recruitment drive for dental surgeons and by the end of the war there were 831 in service.

During his time with 29CCS, Capt. Wilson was kept fully employed. When news of his presence in the Divisional Area reached the men in the trenches, there was a long queue of men clutching dirty handkerchiefs to their mouths outside his surgery tent from morning until nightfall.

Through the first half of September, the Allies continued their unremitting push eastwards; it was not without cost and the two hospitals at Gézaincourt continued to receive a steady flow of casualties, though sick admissions heavily outweighed wounded and dysentery was rife. Rapidly moving troops, whether in advance or retreat, were more prone to this debilitating disease chiefly because thirsty soldiers, whose water bottles had run dry, were inclined to drink from untested water sources rather than wait for the engineers to provide clean, treated water at their new positions. Sanitary arrangements were inevitably more primitive for rapidly moving troops than those in established, dug-in positions.

The US troops in the Divisional Area were particularly afflicted with dysentery; on 22 September, sixty-three Americans, including one officer, were admitted to 29CCS with severe diarrhoea, and during the three weeks from 5–23 September there were 311 cases compared with only eleven wounded from US forces. Coincidentally, during this influx Lt H.R. White of the MORC was attached to the CCS.

As the month progressed there were increasing signs of the Allied successes at the front and staff knew that it would not be long before the hospital was ordered to move forward to a new position. Allied troops had taken Bapaume, and their old hospital site at Grévillers was now occupied by 56CCS, which had already moved forward. The next to move was 3CCS, which had been manning the officers' hospital located in Gézaincourt Chateau, responsibility for which now passed to 29CCS on 13 September. The following day, Brigadier General (Brig. Gen.) L.O.W. Jones, commander of 13th Infantry Brigade, 5th Division, died in the hospital from lobar pneumonia. He was the most senior officer to die in 29CCS during the whole war, but he was buried with exactly the same ceremony and respect which was accorded to the most lowly private soldier.

On 22 September, the CO was advised that the move forward was imminent. The following day was to be the last day for admissions, with all casualties thereafter being diverted to the other Gézaincourt hospital. Then, on the 24th, all patients were to be evacuated and the bulk of the medical staff dispersed.

On the 23rd the last admissions were received; there were 112 patients of the usual polyglot mix of British, American, Chinese, German and British West Indians. There was one death: Coolie Hien Ting Linn of the Chinese Labour Corps, who died of abdominal contusions (accidental).

On Tuesday 24 September the evacuation began: 355 patients were transferred to 21CCS – twelve British officers (sick); 198 British soldiers (sick) and sixteen (wounded); ninety-three American soldiers (sick) and two (wounded); sixteen Chinese coolies (sick); one French officer (sick); one Russian soldier (sick); eleven German POWs (sick); three British West Indian soldiers (sick); and one British and one French civilian. Eight British and one American soldier were returned fit for duty to their units and there was one death – Private Benjamin Skelton (118 US Infantry Regiment), who died of cerebro spinal meningitis. In all, 365 patients had been cleared from the hospital, leaving only forty VD convalescents.

With the patients evacuated, the staff dispersals began: eleven nursing sisters left for temporary duty with No.6 Stationary Hospital; six medical officers, Chaplain J.A. Hogg CF RC, one NCO and thirty-two RAMC soldiers transferred with the patients to 21CCS; one NCO and fifty-three RAMC soldiers transferred to 49CCS; ten RAMC soldiers transferred to 34CCS and two to No.14 Field Ambulance; Air Mechanic 3rd Class J. Morgan RAF, a VD convalescent, was escorted to his base unit under close arrest; and Private R.W. Northover RAMC was transferred sick to 21CCS, from where he was evacuated to base.

The hospital had lost 119 of its staff, leaving the CO, the QM, a skeleton medical staff and 113 RAMC soldiers who, assisted by the thirty-nine faithful VD convalescents, loaded the tents, equipment and stores on to a train at the same time as 21CCS took over their old site and started pitching their tents. The train left the siding at Gézaincourt before nightfall, bound for Wavans, where they were to take over the site recently vacated by 21CCS.

Chapter 7

THE LAST LAP

WEDNESDAY 25 SEPTEMBER 1918
29TH CASUALTY CLEARING STATION,
ROYAL ARMY MEDICAL CORPS,
WAVANS, FRANCE

Wavans is a small village about 10 miles north-west of Doullens, so, in moving there from Gézaincourt, 29CCS was actually moving farther away from the front. But it was only there temporarily to await further orders.

From Wednesday 25 to Saturday 28 September, the casualty clearing station remained parked at Wavans, no longer an operational hospital, with only a skeleton medical staff which was further reduced by the posting of three MOs and thirty RAMC men to 56CCS, and two MOs to 49CCS for temporary duty.

Late on Saturday, the Colonel was advised that a special train would arrive at the Wavans siding the next morning. His orders were to load 29CCS on to this train, which would transport them to their next operational site at Delsaux Farm, near Beugny, about 5 miles to the east of Bapaume.

The area had been overrun by the Germans during their March Offensive, following a gallant defence by the Welsh Regiment, and the area around Delsaux Farm had been heavily fortified by the Germans during their occupation as part of their Beugny-Ytres Defensive Line. It had only been retaken by the British 5th Division on 3 September and, as there had never been a field hospital on the site, it would require extensive preparation on ground heavily scarred by German trenches, shell craters and wire entanglements.

This was the first time in the war that sustained advances had been made by the Allies, necessitating a rapid movement forward of supporting medical services. Gains were being made all along the line and a memorandum issued by DMS Fourth Army suggested the transport likely to be needed for their move:

> Most of the casualty clearing stations which have moved up to date have moved rapidly and at short notice. At first an attempt was made to move casualty clearing stations with twelve lorry loads. The amount of materials, etc., which they could carry on these loads was very limited and quite insufficient to deal with casualties coming in from a big battle. This was stopped and forty lorry loads was allowed. Frequently twenty lorries only were available and they had to make two journeys in one day. This is quite satisfactory provided the distance to move forward is not too great. It is possible for a casualty clearing station with forty lorry loads to close, pack, repitch and open in a new place in thirty-six to forty-eight hours, which means that they carry as essentials all their canvas, Soyer's stoves for cooking, stretchers, blankets, and fifty beds and mattresses, and whatever else the O.C. likes to take to bring the total up to forty loads.

The eighty-three RAMC soldiers remaining on the strength of 29CCS, assisted by the thirty-nine VD convalescents and sixty German POWs which the CO had managed to obtain to assist, started loading the railway wagons as soon as they arrived and had completed the job by 4 p.m. In the event, the tents, equipment and stores of the hospital took twenty closed railway wagons, four open wagons and one flatbed lorry. A locomotive arrived at 7 p.m. and the train moved out of Wavans siding at 7.30 p.m.

Col Carmichael had a personal problem which was causing him considerable concern. His wife and family had been in Malta since February 1914 and his son, Donald, would be 13 years old in six months time. He had been receiving a reasonable preparatory education at a school in Malta, though not as good as he would have received in Britain, but was now at the stage where it was essential he should move on to a British Public School if he was to follow a career in medicine or the Army; and for a family which had served the Crown for 160 years, no other choice was conceivable.

However, German and Austrian submarines had preyed on British shipping in the Mediterranean and there was a grave risk to any family returning to UK by sea; and there were other problems with taking the overland journey through Italy. By September 1918 British losses to U-boat attack had fallen considerably, although they were still active and would remain a threat until the bitter end.*

To add to this was the knowledge that his wife and family had now spent five summers in the blistering heat of Malta; his wife's constitution was not of the strongest and he was anxious for her not to have to spend another summer season there, particularly as the influenza epidemic which was sweeping Europe had already reached the island. Ideally, he would have liked to have taken a month's leave to escort them back personally through Italy and France, but he had sounded out the DMS who had told him that there was no hope of any extended leave with the present activity on the Western Front which, it was hoped, would lead to an early end to the war. In a complete quandary, he decided to ask the advice of a distinguished friend, Col Chesney, who knew the Maltese situation well.

Col Alexander Chesney had commanded battalions of the Worcestershire Regiment both in the Boer War and at the start of the First World War. Now aged 60, he had been 'put out to grass' commanding a battalion of the Royal Defence Corps, the First World War equivalent of the Home Guard. He had married into one of the oldest families of Maltese nobility and his eldest son, Alexander Arthur Ian Austin Chesney Sceberras D'Amico Inguanez, after service in his father's old regiment, in the course of which he was awarded the Military Cross (MC), became the 21st Baron Inguanez, the premier nobleman of Malta, and lived in a beautiful palace in the ancient capital M'dina. Col Chesney wrote:

---

* The British battleship HMS *Britannia* was sunk in the Mediterranean by a U-boat on 9 November 1918, two days before the Armistice.

You have a very difficult decision to make. I entirely agree with you that Hilda should not, if possible, have to spend another summer in Malta. She was looking very drawn when she dined with us in July and the last two seasons have been excessively hot. It is also important that your boy gets to a decent school before he is much older. However, the Bosche submarines are still very active in the Med and it would be foolish to allow her to return by sea even as far as Marseilles. As long as this situation prevails the only sensible course would be to cross to Taranto and then travel overland by rail. In this case, it would be essential for her to travel in company with another Malta family or under the protection of a British officer making the journey. The Italian trains are pretty awful and nobody below the rank of full colonel is allowed to travel in an express train. The best thing, of course, would be if you could get leave to escort the family yourself but I see you are in the thick of it at the moment and your chances of obtaining leave would be pretty slim I imagine.

On balance, Lt Col Carmichael felt that it would be better for them to stay in Malta through the winter when perhaps the war would be won and the shipping routes safe again. It was probably preferable that Donald's education should slip further behind and his wife should take the risk to her health of another Maltese summer, rather than risk the very great danger of a sea trip or the problems which would beset them on the long overland journey. After considerably more thought and soul searching, he wrote to his wife in August:

My own inclination is that you should stay in Malta over the winter and we can then see how things stand at the beginning of the year. If you returned early next year, the boy would only miss one or at most two terms at his new school which would not be disastrous and far better that he should fall a bit behind than that you should all lose your lives. I would dearly like to meet you at Taranto and bring you back myself but I spoke to DMS and he said there was not a hope in hell of my getting leave before Christmas. With the way our forces are surging ahead at the moment it does not look as if the Hun can hold out much longer. Their country is broken and we have heard that they are eating cats and dogs in Berlin.

I would not wish to prejudice any arrangements you may already have made nor to impose my will upon you if you feel very strongly about returning now but, if you do decide to go, you MUST only travel if you have other Malta people going with you. You will have to spend two nights on the train in Italy and it is often impossible to get a sleeping berth with less than 3 or 4 days notice and you could not do this journey in an ordinary compartment with the children. It is also very difficult to get food in Italy so take enough money with you to pay the attendant to get you something at one of the stations.

Don't be tempted to linger in Paris. It is sometimes shelled by the Germans' big guns and allow for the possibility that you may have to spend a few nights in a hotel in a certain seaport before obtaining a cross-channel passage. The ferries are usually full to capacity with servicemen. Remember too that you will be going from the Maltese to the English climate. I am told that coal is in very short supply at home and may be rationed this winter so make sure that you and the children have plenty of warm clothing.

Whatever you ultimately decide, dearest, I have such absolute faith in your judgement and good sense that I will agree but there is one point on which I must lay particular stress – on no account must you travel home by sea other than the crossing to Taranto.

The train carrying 29CCS arrived at the Delsaux Farm siding at 12.30 p.m. on Monday 30 September and unloading started immediately. As the Colonel had feared, the ground had been badly cut up by German defensive positions and the heavy fighting which had been necessary for the British forces to overrun them. The farm itself was a substantial group of adjoining buildings in a U shape, which the Germans had fortified on the three closed sides with trenches and barbed wire. The fourth open side faced the main Beugny to Havrincourt road, with the railway siding on the other side running parallel to the road.

Much site clearance and levelling was required before the RAMC soldiers and their thirty-nine VD convalescent helpers could start pitching the camp. The hospital was non-operational for three and a half days until 4 October, during which period the medical staff started returning. On 1 October, three MOs and thirty-one RAMC men arrived, and a water cart reported for temporary duty from Third Army Water

Tank Company, Royal Engineers. On the 4th the first four patients were admitted, two sick and two wounded, and one surgical team, thirteen nursing sisters and sixty-five RAMC soldiers joined the strength. The following day forty-eight patients were admitted, a further two surgical teams arrived and the first death occurred – Private R. Bradley (9th King's Liverpool Regiment). Preparation of a convenient burial ground for the hospital had presented great difficulties in view of the German trenches and a site was not yet ready. Private Bradley's body was therefore taken to the old burial ground at Grévillers.

Casualty clearing stations in the busy sectors usually operated in pairs. At times of great activity, one of the pair, when overwhelmed with casualties, could close temporarily and divert its admissions to the other. Where appropriate, the COs could also agree upon a temporary screening policy, so, for example, all surgical cases could be sent to the CCS with the greater theatre capacity; or contagious cases could be taken by the CCS which had established an appropriate quarantine area. The arrival at Delsaux Farm of 46CCS from Le Bac de Sud on 7 October, coupled with the augmentation of their own personnel over the past few days, suggested to the staff of 29CCS that another major engagement was imminent.

They were not mistaken. On Tuesday 8 October, a massive attack along a 20-mile front was launched by the British Third and Fourth Armies, with the US 30th Division and the French Army to the south. There were significant gains along the whole front, but they were not lightly won; the fighting was extremely fierce and casualties very heavy. On the Third Army front, 29CCS and 46CCS at Delsaux Farm, and 3CCS (Canadian) and 18CCS at Ytres, were the most forward, about 10 miles behind the front, and received the bulk of casualties in the initial phases of the offensive. During the first day, 29CCS admitted 475 British and eighty-seven German wounded. There were ten deaths in the hospital that day, and twenty-four the following day. In the initial attack, the preponderance of casualties came from 2nd Division and 3rd Division of VI Corps, but as the battle progressed, every division was to make its sacrifice.

Typical of the action that day were the activities of the 63rd (RN) Division of XVII Corps. The division included four battalions (Anson, Drake, Hawke and Hood) of sailors and one of Royal Marines fighting as infantry soldiers; it had been formed in September 1914, initially from Royal Marines and Naval Reservists for whom no ship was available and, though it retained naval ranks and many naval traditions, its men had fought in the trenches as infantry throughout the war. The division was heavily involved in the first attack.

During the night of 7/8 October, 189 Brigade, comprising Drake, Hawke and Hood Battalions, and a Light Trench Mortar Battery, moved into position north-east of Rumilly for a dawn attack on a German defensive position at Niergnies, near Cambrai. Drake Battalion and 2nd Royal Irish Regiment led the assault at 4.30 a.m. and had secured the German frontline position by 6 a.m. Hood Battalion and the Royal Marine Battalion then advanced through them and had captured the village and the enemy positions behind it by 8 a.m. At 9.30 a.m. German infantry, supported by seven tanks they had captured from the British, launched a strong counter-attack.

Twenty-one-year-old Sub-Lieutenant (Sub-Lt) Jack Clifford Morley was commanding a section of Hood Battalion and, seeing the approaching tanks, directed a captured German field gun to be brought into action against them. The sailors destroyed one of the tanks, but the other six got through and there was heavy hand-to-hand fighting throughout the morning. After several more enemy counter-attacks, and a bombardment from 223 and 317 Brigades RFA, the supporting artillery, the division pressed on and had secured a position just outside Cambrai by nightfall.

During the day the sailors had taken 1,200 prisoners and had captured nine artillery pieces and eighty-one machine guns. The cost had been high, however: seventy-three men had been killed and 540 wounded, including Sub-Lt Morley who had received a serious wound to his left side. He was transported by ambulance to Delsaux Farm and was one of thirty British officers admitted to 29CCS that day. He was no stranger to military hospitals, having received grievous wounds in Gallipoli in his right arm, head, chest, back and legs. After initial surgery in a CCS, he had been evacuated to England where he had spent seven months during 1916 in a military hospital. He was commissioned on 29 May 1918 and had taken up his first appointment as an officer in Hood Battalion on 1 October. Eight days later, after extensive attention from one of the surgical teams at 29CCS, he was struggling for life in a bed in the post-operative ward next to Sub-Lt Orlando Harris of Hawke Battalion, who had been severely wounded in the same action.

Jack Morley was a strong young man who had been a keen sportsman and cricketer in his hometown of Stockport before the war. But his poor body had hardly recovered from its previous injuries and this latest trauma was more than it could take. He died two days later on 10 October and is buried at Delsaux Farm alongside Sub-Lt Harris, Petty Officers (PO) Johnston and Russell, Leading Seamen (L/Sea.) Athroll and Gardner, Able Seamen (AB) Clark, Cotton and Laird, and Royal Marines Crook and Nicolle, all of the RN Division, who died on the same day.

In the first week of the offensive, from 8–14 October, 1,483 British patients were admitted to 29CCS, plus a considerable number of Germans. On the 9th the British took Cambrai and, on the following day, Le Cateau. The Hindenburg Line, the Germans' last and most strongly fortified defensive line, had now been breached along its entire length – a major blow to enemy morale. The Americans and French were making excellent progress in the south and the Allies were steadily gaining ground all along the front. The nature of the war was reverting daily to one of mobility and open-ground tactics, which had not been seen since the early months of the war when both sides had dug in for three and a half years of trench-bound deadlock.

On 22 October the British took Valenciennes and the following day launched another major offensive on a line from Valenciennes to Le Cateau, bringing with it another surge in battlefield casualties. As the Allies rolled forward, an increasing number of German wounded had to be left behind by their own medical services and the percentage of German officers and men admitted to the forward field hospitals increased daily.

This added to the general abatement of spirit in the German Army, which was losing ground steadily. Morale had deteriorated sharply since the euphoria of its successes in March. Many sections of their troops had lost heart and were surrendering in their thousands, but for others this merely strengthened their resolve as they put up a fiercer resistance to the Allied advance. The final weeks of fighting, as the casualty figures on both sides show, was as savage and determined as at any other time in the war.

As the British line advanced, the CCSs at Delsaux Farm and Ytres, the nearest to the front at the beginning of October, were leapfrogged by medical units in the rear moving up into the newly taken areas. However, with the inevitable transport difficulties in a landscape which had been recently destroyed by artillery bombardment and prolonged infantry conflict, some of the newly advanced hospitals could not immediately be serviced by ambulance trains and casualties had to be passed back to Delsaux Farm and Ytres by motor ambulance convoys. There was consequently no easing of pressure on these two hospitals, which, at the busiest times, had to pass casualties back to the CCSs at Grévillers and Beaulencourt. Awoingt, the site of the newly arrived 28CCS, 45CCS and 59CCS, was an example: with no trains able to get through to Cambrai, casualties brought in to Awoingt had to be transported to Delsaux Farm and Ytres for evacuation to the rear. During peak fighting periods, ten ambulance cars were leaving Awoingt for Delsaux Farm and Ytres every hour, day and night – one every six minutes. On 25 October 29CCS admitted 171 sick and 543 British wounded, as well as ninety-eight German wounded.

The speed of the British advance was so great that it often confounded DMS's carefully planned strategy to keep medical support as close behind the frontline as possible. Towards the end of October, three casualty clearing stations, 19CCS, 3CCS and 21CCS, had been moved up to Caudry, midway between Cambrai and Le Cateau, just behind the frontline, where good buildings were available.

Another great Allied offensive was due to commence on 4 November and the hospitals were ready for the usual surge of casualties and for their rapid evacuation by rail. Then, on Sunday 3 November, the bridge at Caudry was blown up by a delayed-action mine and no ambulance trains could reach the hospitals. Twenty buses were acquired and, when the battle commenced, they ran a continuous shuttle service to Awoingt, Ytres and Delsaux Farm. With shell-cratered roads and frequent blockages, it was a long and uncomfortable journey for the unfortunate patients.

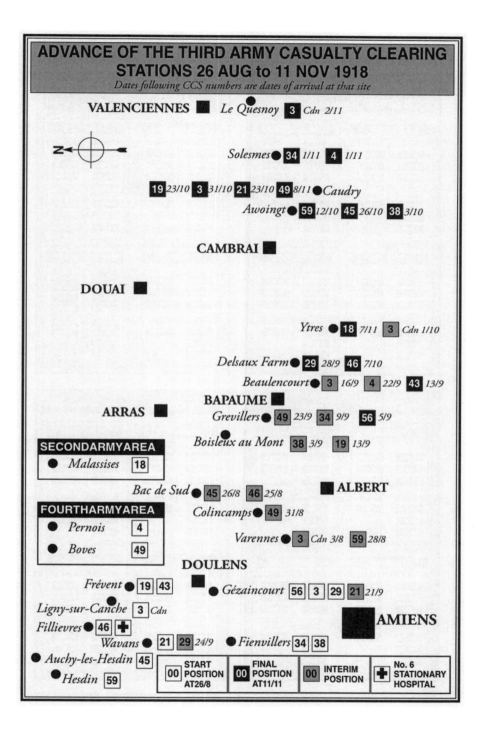

ADVANCE OF THE THIRD ARMY CASUALTY CLEARING STATIONS 26 AUG to 11 NOV 1918

Dates following CCS numbers are dates of arrival at that site

VALENCIENNES ■ Le Quesnoy **3** Cdn 2/11

N

Solesmes **34** 1/11 **4** 1/11

19 23/10 **3** 31/10 **21** 23/10 **49** 8/11 Caudry

Awoingt **59** 12/10 **45** 26/10 **38** 3/10

CAMBRAI ■

DOUAI ■

Ytres **18** 7/11 **3** Cdn 1/10

Delsaux Farm **29** 28/9 **46** 7/10

Beaulencourt **3** 16/9 **4** 22/9 **43** 13/9

BAPAUME ■

ARRAS ■   Grevillers **49** 23/9 **34** 9/9 **56** 5/9

Boisleux au Mont **38** 3/9 **19** 13/9

SECONDARMYAREA
● Malassises **18**

Bac de Sud **45** 26/8 **46** 25/8   ■ ALBERT

FOURTHARMYAREA   Colincamps **49** 31/8
● Pernois **4**
● Boves **49**   Varennes **3** Cdn 3/8 **59** 28/8

DOULENS ■

Frévent **19** **43**   ● Gézaincourt **56** **3** **29** **21** 21/9

Ligny-sur-Canche **3** Cdn   AMIENS
Fillievres **46** ✚
Wavans **21** **29** 24/9   ● Fienvillers **34** **38**
● Auchy-les-Hesdin **45**
● Hesdin **59**

| **00** START POSITION AT26/8 | **00** FINAL POSITION AT11/11 | **00** INTERIM POSITION | ✚ No. 6 STATIONARY HOSPITAL |

THE BRITISH THIRD ARMY

at 11 November 1918
General Hon. Sir Julian H. G. Byng

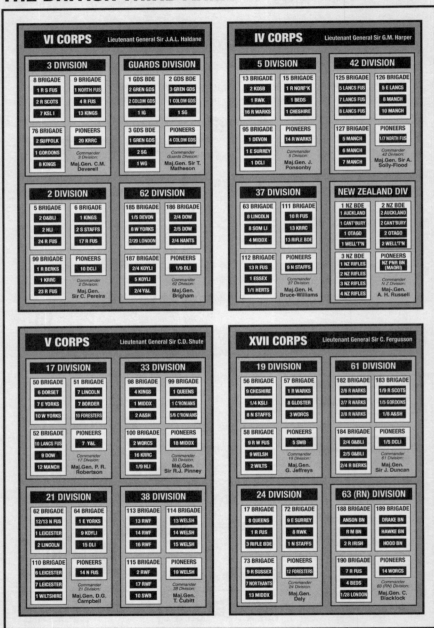

VI CORPS — Lieutenant General Sir J.A.L. Haldane

3 DIVISION

8 BRIGADE	9 BRIGADE
1 R S FUS	1 NORTH FUS
2 R SCOTS	4 R FUS
7 KSLI	13 KINGS

76 BRIGADE	PIONEERS
2 SUFFOLK	20 KRRC
1 GORDONS	Commander 3 Division:
8 KINGS	Maj.Gen. C.M. Deverell

GUARDS DIVISION

1 GDS BDE	2 GDS BDE
2 GREN GDS	3 GREN GDS
2 COLDM GDS	1 COLDM GDS
1 IG	1 SG

3 GDS BDE	PIONEERS
1 GREN GDS	4 COLDM GDS
2 SG	Commander Guards Division:
1 WG	Maj.Gen. Sir T. Matheson

2 DIVISION

5 BRIGADE	6 BRIGADE
2 O&BLI	1 KINGS
2 HLI	2 S STAFFS
24 R FUS	17 R FUS

99 BRIGADE	PIONEERS
1 R BERKS	10 DCLI
1 KRRC	Commander 2 Division:
23 R FUS	Maj.Gen. Sir C. Pereira

62 DIVISION

185 BRIGADE	186 BRIGADE
1/5 DEVON	2/4 DOW
8 W YORKS	2/5 DOW
2/20 LONDON	2/4 HANTS

187 BRIGADE	PIONEERS
2/4 KOYLI	1/9 DLI
5 KOYLI	Commander 62 Division:
2/4 Y&L	Maj.Gen. Brigham

IV CORPS — Lieutenant General Sir G.M. Harper

5 DIVISION

13 BRIGADE	15 BRIGADE
2 KOSB	1 R NORF'K
1 RWK	1 BEDS
16 R WARKS	1 CHESHIRE

95 BRIGADE	PIONEERS
1 DEVON	14 R WARKS
1 E SURREY	Commander 5 Division:
1 DCLI	Maj.Gen. J. Ponsonby

42 DIVISION

125 BRIGADE	126 BRIGADE
5 LANCS FUS	5 E LANCS
7 LANCS FUS	8 MANCH
8 LANCS FUS	10 MANCH

127 BRIGADE	PIONEERS
5 MANCH	1/7 NORTH FUS
6 MANCH	Commander 42 Division:
7 MANCH	Maj.Gen. Sir A. Solly-Flood

37 DIVISION

63 BRIGADE	111 BRIGADE
8 LINCOLN	10 R FUS
8 SOM LI	13 KRRC
4 MIDDX	13 RIFLE BDE

112 BRIGADE	PIONEERS
13 R FUS	9 N STAFFS
1 ESSEX	Commander 37 Division:
1/1 HERTS	Maj.Gen. H. Bruce-Williams

NEW ZEALAND DIV

1 NZ BDE	2 NZ BDE
1 AUCKLAND	2 AUCKLAND
1 CANT'BURY	2 CANT'BURY
1 OTAGO	2 OTAGO
1 WELL'T'N	2 WELL'T'N

3 NZ BDE	PIONEERS
1 NZ RIFLES	NZ PNR BN (MAORI)
2 NZ RIFLES	Commander N Z Division:
3 NZ RIFLES	Maj.-Gen. A. H. Russell
4 NZ RIFLES	

V CORPS — Lieutenant General Sir C.D. Shute

17 DIVISION

50 BRIGADE	51 BRIGADE
6 DORSET	7 LINCOLN
7 E YORKS	7 BORDER
10 W YORKS	10 FORESTERS

52 BRIGADE	PIONEERS
10 LANCS FUS	7 Y&L
9 DOW	Commander 17 Division:
12 MANCH	Maj.Gen. P. R. Robertson

33 DIVISION

98 BRIGADE	99 BRIGADE
4 KINGS	1 QUEENS
1 MIDDX	1 C'RONIANS
2 A&SH	5/6 C'RONIANS

100 BRIGADE	PIONEERS
2 WORCS	18 MIDDX
16 KRRC	Commander 33 Division:
1/9 HLI	Maj.Gen. Sir R.J. Pinney

21 DIVISION

62 BRIGADE	64 BRIGADE
12/13 N FUS	1 E YORKS
1 LEICESTER	9 KOYLI
2 LINCOLN	15 DLI

110 BRIGADE	PIONEERS
6 LEICESTER	14 N FUS
7 LEICESTER	Commander 21 Division:
1 WILTSHIRE	Maj.Gen. D.G. Campbell

38 DIVISION

113 BRIGADE	114 BRIGADE
13 RWF	13 WELSH
14 RWF	14 WELSH
16 RWF	15 WELSH

115 BRIGADE	PIONEERS
2 RWF	19 WELSH
17 RWF	Commander 38 Division:
10 SWB	Maj.Gen. T. Cubitt

XVII CORPS — Lieutenant General Sir C. Fergusson

19 DIVISION

56 BRIGADE	57 BRIGADE
9 CHESHIRE	1 R WARKS
1/4 KSLI	8 GLOSTER
8 N STAFFS	3 WORCS

58 BRIGADE	PIONEERS
9 R W FUS	5 SWB
9 WELSH	Commander 19 Division:
2 WILTS	Maj.Gen. G. Jeffreys

61 DIVISION

182 BRIGADE	183 BRIGADE
2/6 R WARKS	1/9 R SCOTS
2/7 R WARKS	1/5 GORDONS
2/8 R WARKS	1/8 A&SH

184 BRIGADE	PIONEERS
2/4 O&BLI	1/5 DCLI
2/5 O&BLI	Commander 61 Division:
2/4 R BERKS	Maj.Gen. Sir J. Duncan

24 DIVISION

17 BRIGADE	72 BRIGADE
8 QUEENS	9 E SURREY
1 R FUS	8 RWK
3 RIFLE BDE	1 N STAFFS

73 BRIGADE	PIONEERS
9 R SUSSEX	12 FORESTERS
7 NORTHANTS	Commander 24 Division:
13 MIDDX	Maj.Gen. Daly

63 (RN) DIVISION

188 BRIGADE	189 BRIGADE
ANSON BN	DRAKE BN
R M BN	HAWKE BN
2 R IRISH	HOOD BN

190 BRIGADE	PIONEERS
7 R FUS	14 WORCS
4 BEDS	Commander 63 (RN) Division:
1/28 LONDON	Maj.Gen. C. Blacklock

Chapter 8

VICTORY!

On Monday 4 November 1918 the Western Front once again trembled with the violence of a heavy artillery bombardment before the infantry divisions of Britain and her allies surged ahead in what was to be the final great offensive of the war. The British First, Third and Fourth Armies attacked along a 30-mile front from west of the River Scheldt at Valenciennes to Guise on the River Oise, reaching a point east of Le Quesnoy. The Americans advanced to Stenay on the River Meuse, the French reached the Ardennes Canal at Le Chesne, and the Belgians entered the north-western and southern suburbs of Ghent.

Throughout the day, the twenty Caudry buses ferried casualties to Awoingt, Ytres and Delsaux Farm, and by evening the drivers were exhausted. The CO at 29CCS eased their situation by sending one of his surgical teams, comprising Lt J.B. Flick and Lt I.B. Roberts of the US Army, an Australian nursing sister and two American orderlies, as emergency reinforcements to the hard-pressed hospitals at Caudry. More casualties could consequently receive surgery nearer to the front, although there were still problems in getting them evacuated to base. As well as no trains getting through to Caudry, the trains to Awoingt were running very erratically and in insufficient numbers to clear the volume of wounded arriving hourly to the three hospitals there, both direct from the ADSs and RAPs in the frontline, and from transfers brought in by the Caudry buses. The evacuation had therefore to be augmented with large numbers of ambulance cars.

During the fighting on 4 and 5 November, 473 British, ninety-eight Germans, one American, plus a few French and Russians were admitted to 29CCS. During the same two days the Third Army took 10,000 prisoners and captured 200 guns. The Colonel wrote:

This must be very brief as we are all working round the clock receiving the wounded from what must surely be the final battle of the War. The Germans are collapsing everywhere. They are surrendering in their thousands and very glad to be out of it. At least as prisoners they receive some food. We are in a place far advanced from our last location which I will tell you when we are allowed. It is much closer to the front although each day the sound of the guns gets slightly fainter as our troops in front of us press ahead at a great pace. I have not had a chance to look around the area as we have been kept constantly busy in setting up the hospital and caring for a large volume of casualties from both sides.... I could not wish for a better, more dedicated team of doctors, nurses and orderlies.

By 6 November the Germans' main lateral line of communication had been severed by the Allies, and the German Army was in general retreat from the Scheldt to the Meuse. The British were advancing to Maubeuge, Avesnes and to Mons in Belgium where it had all started in 1914. The French captured Vervins and Rethel on the Aisne, and the Americans entered Sedan. On the same day, Gen. von Gündell, State-Secretary Erzberger, Count Oberndorff, Gen. von Winterfeld and Capt. von Selow of the German Navy left Berlin for France to discuss the terms of the proposed Armistice with the Allies. As they were driven, in a heavily guarded convoy, across the devastated landscape of Northern France, where hardly a building or a tree was left standing and where fields and lanes merged together into an endless homogenous expanse of shell-cratered desolation, the German delegates had ample opportunity to reflect upon the results of their aggression.

034 The 'Hospital Valley' at Gézaincourt in which two, and sometimes three, casualty clearing stations were located. The area resembled "a vast tented city".

035 The disused railway halt at Gézaincourt from where a continuous succession of Ambulance Trains evacuated wounded to base hospitals, having received treatment and emergency surgery at the CCSs in the valley. The Cross of Sacrifice in Bagneux CWGC Cemetery can be seen on the left.

036 The grave of Private R.G. Crompton, West Yorkshire Regiment, who was buried in the Bagneux Cemetery, Gézaincourt on 25 April 1918. He was aged 19. The official photograph taken in the early 1920s, showing the original wooden cross, and sent to the family when they requested details. © Wellcome Library, London

037 The same grave today. © Richard Crompton

038 A photograph of Private J.W. Laurenson, Durham Light Infantry, who died of wounds in 29CCS on 27 August 1918. The photograph was left recently with the Cemetery Visitors' Book by a relative visiting the site.

039 A view of the Bagneux CWGC Cemetery at Gézaincourt with the "Hospital Valley" beyond.

040 Graves of two Coolies of the Chinese Labour Corps.

041 Graves of the Canadian Medical personnel killed in the German raid on the hospital at Doullens.

042 RAMC ambulances collect the wounded from a battlefield.

043 Soldiers struggle to free an ambulance stuck in the mud.

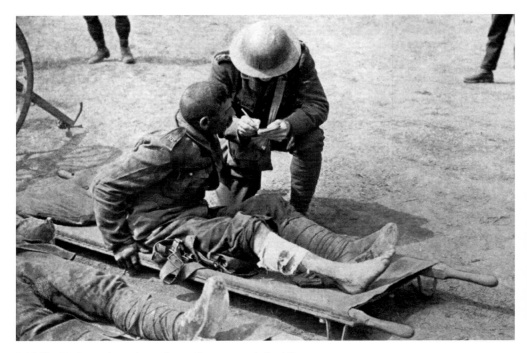

044 The Padre writes a letter home for a wounded soldier.

045 Personnel of 29th Casualty Clearing Station, Germany 1919. The CO is in an overcoat sitting between the Chaplain and the Quartermaster.

046 The French hospice at Warloy-Baillon where the officers of 29CCS slept on the floor of the porter's lodge during their retreat from Grévillers on 25 March 1918.

047 29th Casualty Clearing Station Bonn, 1919. A ward in the converted chapel.
© Imperial War Museum (Q3747)

048 The 19th century St. Marien's Hospital in Bonn in which 29CCS was located.
© Imperial War Museum (Q3746)

They were conducted to a railway carriage in a clearing in the Forest of Compiègne in which the talks were to take place. The Germans had hoped for some mitigation of the harsh terms demanded by the French, but soon realised that there was to be no negotiation: unlike the Americans and the British whose proposals showed greater clemency, the French had suffered four years of occupation and the destruction of a large part of their country, and wanted nothing less than total restitution and the humiliation of the enemy.* It was a 'take it or leave it' situation.

There was, in fact, no 'leave it' option for the Germans either. On 29/30 October the German Navy at Wilhelmshaven had mutinied and their disaffection had spread across the whole country. On 9 November it was announced that Kaiser Wilhelm II had abdicated and Germany was proclaimed a republic. Two days later, at 4 a.m. on Monday 11 November, the Armistice was signed by both sides, who agreed, and decreed, that hostilities should cease at 11 a.m. the same day.

The run-up to the ceasefire saw some of the fiercest and most determined fighting of the war. Allied commanders knew that from 11 a.m. they would not be permitted to advance any further and were anxious to gain as much ground as they possibly could in the remaining time, and to secure a position which would be convenient for their post-war logistical requirements. Many also felt that the plans for a ceasefire might fall through, in which case the enemy would undoubtedly take full advantage of any relaxation or reduced vigilance on the part of the Allied forces. Casualties continued to arrive at the hospitals at Delsaux Farm until the last moment.

---

* A reciprocal act of humiliation took place on 22 June 1941 when the Germans insisted that the French should sign their surrender in the same railway carriage in exactly the same place in the Forest of Compiègne. The Kaiser, who had fled into exile in the Netherlands from where the Dutch refused all attempts to extradite him, missed seeing this ritual reported as he had died seventeen days earlier on 5 June.

Mrs Hilda Carmichael had decided that, no matter what the difficulties or discomforts, the family must return from Malta to Britain to enable Donald to start at his Public School for the new academic year. By the time she received her husband's letter on the subject at the end of August, she had already been in communication with the Imperial Service College and arranged for a place for Donald to start in September. The school had moved from Westward Ho! in North Devon to Windsor since her husband and his brother had attended.

As her husband had asked, she booked passage on the steamer to Taranto and arranged to make the journey with an Army padre's wife and her two little girls. The journey through Italy was a nightmare: having waited for two days in a dirty little hotel in Taranto, the only beds they could find in the town, they managed to secure berths in adjacent compartments on the train leaving for Rome, Genoa and Marseilles the next day. There were no porters at the station so the families had to struggle with their own luggage, which was copious, despite their heavy trunks having been sent on ahead as freight. To add to the discomfort of the journey, three out of the four children had caught fleas in the hotel beds and, in a confined space, without facilities to bathe or wash clothes, it was not long before they had spread to everyone else.

The journey was stop-start all the way, the train sometimes stopping for several hours at a time. As Col Chesney had warned, obtaining food was the passengers' responsibility and, when the train reached any station where food was available, the crush of passengers struggling to get to the food stall was intolerable and there was no sign of the attendant. Their salvation came in the form of a huge bombardier of the Royal Garrison Artillery (RGA) whose name has, sadly, not been recorded but the children christened him 'Tommy'. Tommy, recognising the plight of the two women, became their guardian angel for the journey, keeping the children endlessly entertained during the day, heaving suitcases up and down from luggage racks when required and helping the families in many different ways. At something like 6ft 6in and, perhaps, 20 stone in weight, Tommy was not a man with whom other men tended to argue and he had no difficulty in obtaining food for them all or in securing porters for the ladies at the end of the dreadful journey which took three days to Marseilles, a further two days to Boulogne on the

French railway system, which was slightly better, and then a night in Boulogne before getting a ferry across the Channel to Dover.

At Victoria Station, Hilda and the children said goodbye to the padre's family and to Tommy, who was travelling on to his home in Yorkshire. They thanked him profusely and he refused adamantly to accept any sort of present from them. They got a taxi to the flat, 48 Talgarth Mansions, West Kensington, which Hilda's father had bought on his return from India.

While the armies of the world had, over the past four years, been enacting the greatest man-made disaster of all time, nature was preparing to launch the greatest natural disaster in the form of a particularly virulent type of influenza which attacked, in the main, strong, healthy young adults. The flu pandemic reached every corner of the world, infecting around 500 million and killing between 50 and 100 million. Within days of her arrival in London, Hilda had fallen victim to it and was seriously ill for several weeks. Had it not been for the care and medical skill of her father, it is probable she would have been one of the victims.

On the final day of the war, it was business as usual for 29 CCS and there was no record of the Armistice in the War Diary. Admissions comprised the usual mixed bag of British, Chinese, British West Indian, Indian, French and German troops. There were four deaths at Delsaux Farm on the 11th: Private Ernest Francis Brooks (2nd/6th Royal Warwicks), aged 19; Private Wilford Henry Carver (7th Somerset Light Infantry), aged 21; Pioneer Duncan Reginald Colema (Royal Engineers), aged 25; and Private J. Millington (9th King's Own Yorkshire Light Infantry), whose age was not known. Stories abound of the fighting during the last few hours of the war and there have been several claimants for the macabre honour of being the last man killed. It is now generally conceded that Private George Lawrence Price of the 2nd Canadian Division, who was shot by a German sniper at 10.58 a.m. during heavy fighting in the village of Havré, was the last soldier of the British Empire to be killed. The final honour, though, is taken by Private Henry Gunther, an American of German descent who, it was said, had suffered abuse throughout his life because of his German blood and was eager to prove his patriotism. At one minute to 11 a.m., he got up and charged towards a German machine-gun emplacement. The astonished Germans shouted at him and waved at him to go back, there were only seconds left, but he kept going. The German machine gun fired five shots which stopped him in his tracks and, it is said, that as he fell dead to the ground, the guns stopped and silence enveloped the Western Front.

From Armistice Day, admissions to 29CCS fell away sharply. The last three 'wounded' casualties, one officer and two soldiers, were received on the 12th and, from then to the end of November, 'sick' admissions were, on average, only four or five a day. With the frantic activity during the last three months of the war, leave had fallen very behind and the CO saw this slack period as an ideal time to start catching up. He also knew that with so few admissions it would not be long before orders would come for a move; 46CCS moved out on 18 November, leaving 29CCS as the only hospital at Delsaux Farm. A leave rota was drawn up to allow about half the personnel immediate leave, with the other half going on their return.

On 18 November, Lt Col Carmichael left on two weeks' UK leave via Boulogne. Both the children were by now at their boarding schools and Hilda was still at Talgarth Mansions convalescing under the care of her father, Lt Col James Armstrong of the IMS. Now the war was over, Lt Col Carmichael was hopeful that his next appointment would be in the UK as he had served nearly five years overseas in Malta and France. With this in mind, he wanted to see Hilda and the children settled into suitable temporary accommodation until he returned, and was allocated a married quarter on his new station. After inspecting several places, they decided upon a suite of rooms in a small private hotel in Southsea with five or six elderly and genteel residents including a retired officer and two officers' widows, with whom, they felt, they would have much in common. Having arranged for their furniture to be placed in store, James moved them into their new home and saw them settled before he had to return to France.

Donald had settled in well at the Imperial Service College, was proving a useful winger on the rugby field and was clearly enjoying the harsh life at a Public School preparing boys for imperial military service. He wrote to his father:

We have to wash in cold water every morning at 7.15 am stripped down to the waist and I heartily agree there is nothing that so refreshes and takes the sleepy feeling away so much as to duck your head into a basin of cold water when you first get up. On Wednesdays and Saturdays we have a cold shower which is equally invigorating.... We are fed very well. For breakfast we have two plates of porridge, some meat, as much bread as we like and a cup of tea. For lunch meat and pudding. For tea bread and butter, a cup of tea and perhaps some cake. For supper bread and butter.... Every Sunday we are allowed to go into the barracks and listen to the band of the Life Guards. It is very nice and sometimes the soldiers let us go round the stables and give the horses sugar which we get at the College from the Chef or one of the cooks.

The Colonel returned to France on 4 December in the company of one of his officers, Capt. W.J.B. Selkirk. On his arrival he was told by his second-in-command, Maj. R.B. Roe, that admissions had diminished further and DMS had already started transferring some of the medical staff to other hospitals. They had already lost two MOs and five nursing sisters, and on 10 December twenty RAMC soldiers were transferred to 56CCS. On 16 December four more sisters were posted away and orders were received from DMS Third Army for the hospital to close for all admissions as from the following day.

On 18 December the remaining soldiers started striking canvas, which continued through the week before Christmas, impeded by continuous heavy rain, until on the 22nd the CO halted the work to await a dry spell. A guard was placed upon the stores and equipment already stacked beside the railway line, and the piles of boxes were covered over with tarpaulins. The rain continued until Boxing Day. The soldiers, having enjoyed a general holiday on Christmas Day with such merriment as they could muster, now got down to the task of drying out the vast acreage of canvas. Some of the marquees had to be re-pitched to give them a chance to dry out; to have stored them wet would have resulted in mould and rot.

On Saturday 28 December, eight NCOs and soldiers, including the doughty Sgt Rowe, were struck off the strength of 29CCS and proceeded to Cambrai for interview for early release as coal miners, which were badly needed in UK to keep the home fires burning. The Colonel was very sorry to lose Sgt Rowe, who had been with him since he first took command of 29CCS and had become one of his most dependable NCOs.

On the 30th the rain stopped and two days of fair weather enabled the men to complete the drying out and packing up of the struck marquees in which the wards, operating theatres and treatment areas had been located. This left the accommodation and mess tents, cookhouse, wash and storage houses to be packed up when orders to move were received.

The hospital remained on site at Delsaux Farm for the first three weeks of 1919, closed and with no activity other than routine postings and leave movements. On 14 January DMS Third Army advised the CO that a move was imminent and asked for weights of stores and equipment, and the number of railway carriages required. He replied: 'Ordnance approx 50 tons; Medical Stores 2 tons; Truckage required 25 covered, 4 open and one flat wagon'. Then, at 7.50 a.m. on 20 January, a train arrived with orders for the unit to load for transportation to Calais. The following day the CO obtained a working party of fifty POWs to assist with striking the remainder of the camp and loading the train. They worked from 8 a.m. to 4 p.m. on the 21st and 22nd, and at 5 p.m. the CO reported that the hospital was fully loaded and ready to depart. DMS then ordered that the CO, the QM and twenty-five soldiers should act as guards and accompany the train to Calais. The sergeant major was to proceed to 18CCS and all remaining men to No.6 Stationary Hospital. Maj. Roe was transferred to 19CCS and the two padres, Revd R. Holme and Revd A.L. Nixon to Dieppe and XVII Corps Heavy Artillery respectively. All NCOs and men presently on detached duties were to remain with their present units until further notice.

At 10 p.m. on 22 January the train left Delsaux Farm for Calais, where it arrived on Friday 24th. It was shunted into Cologne Garage and the CO reported their arrival to ADMS Calais. The following day they were shunted to the ordnance siding at Beaumarais, where they remained on the train for the next three days awaiting orders.

At 6.40 p.m. on Tuesday 28 January orders were received by 21CCS and 29CCS to hand over all stores and equipment, but to keep all records and be ready to move out for Bonn, in Germany, at very short notice. The 21CCS train drew up alongside them and unloading and handing over stores to the ordnance depot started at 8 a.m. the next day. This was complete by Friday 31st, except for one railway wagon containing 3,000 blankets which had been detached from the train in error by the rail transport officer (RTO) at Fontinette. Late on the 31st the CO reported to ADMS Calais that all ordnance, engineer and medical stores and equipment had been handed over, with the exception of the blanket truck which the RTO at Fontinette would return, and that 29CCS was ready to move.

For the next three days the train sat in a siding at Calais awaiting orders. Living in box cars in mid-winter was not only uncomfortable but extremely cold. One carriage acted as an improvised cookhouse and storeroom, and in the cars where the men ate, slept and spent all their free time, packing cases served as chairs and tables. Each car had a coal-burning stove with its chimney poking through the roof of the carriage. The men huddled round the stoves to get what warmth they could, wrote letters home and tried to catch up on their sleep. The Colonel wrote to Donald:

> I am very pleased that you are doing so well at rugger and shooting but it is very, very important, old chap, that you also make good progress with your school work. Through no fault of your own this wretched war has put you behind your fellow pupils in basic education and you must now work doubly hard to try and catch them up. It is very hard on you, I know, but your whole future life will depend on what you manage to achieve during these next four years so it will really be worth the hard slog in the end. I know you can do it and will work very hard to make your mother and me proud of you. I will really look forward to coming to one of your rugger matches when I am next back on leave.

At one minute past midnight on Wednesday 5 February the train left Calais and arrived at Bonn at 1 p.m. on Friday 7th. Transport was waiting to take them to the building where 1CCS (Canadian) was operating. Lt Col A.E.H. Bennett CAMC, officer commanding 1CCS (Canadian) recorded in his War Diary:

> Advance party of 29CCS arrived today at 4.30 pm – OC Lieutenant-Colonel Carmichael and his Quartermaster and 25 other ranks – a big change for them after being 16 days in box cars.

Lt Col Carmichael's orders stated that his own personnel would be rejoining the unit shortly and, when he was up to strength, 29CCS should relieve the Canadians.

The return of personnel started on Tuesday 11th with the arrival of five MOs, and RSM Charlesworth with forty-eight RAMC NCOs and men. Now able to operate as a hospital again, 29CCS took over from the Canadians, including their stores, equipment and patients, who comprised sixty British officers and men, plus two Serbians. On the same day they had twenty-two new admissions. 29CCS was back in business!

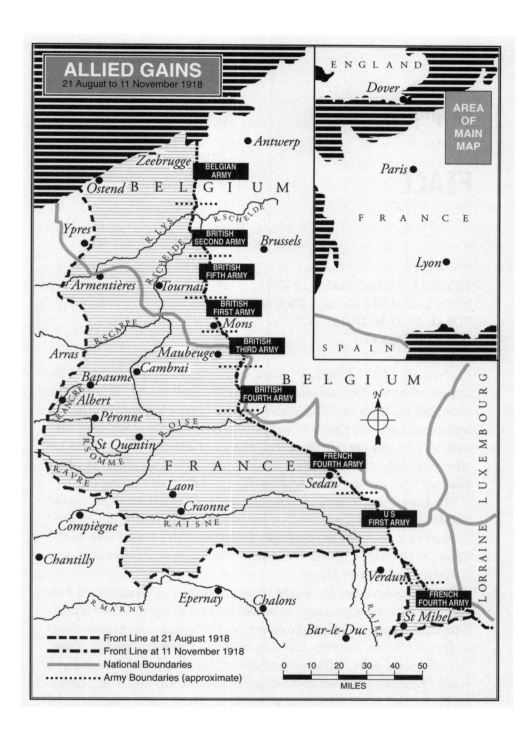

ALLIED GAINS
21 August to 11 November 1918

ENGLAND

Dover

AREA
OF
MAIN
MAP

Antwerp

Paris

BELGIAN
ARMY

Zeebrugge

FRANCE

Ostend B E L G I U M

R.SCHELDE

Ypres

BRITISH
SECOND ARMY

Brussels

R. LYS

Lyon

BRITISH
FIFTH ARMY

R.SCHELDE

Armentières

Tournai

BRITISH
FIRST ARMY

B.SCARPE

Mons

SPAIN

BRITISH
THIRD ARMY

Arras

Maubeuge

Cambrai

B E L G I U M

Bapaume

BRITISH
FOURTH ARMY

Albert

R.ANCRE

Péronne

R.OISE

St Quentin

R.SOMME

F R A N C E

FRENCH
FOURTH ARMY

R.AVRE

Laon

Sedan

Craonne

Compiègne

R. AISNE

US
FIRST ARMY

Chantilly

LORRAINE LUXEMBOURG

Verdun

FRENCH
FOURTH ARMY

Epernay

Chalons

St Mihel

R.MARNE

R.AIRE

Bar-le-Duc

- - - Front Line at 21 August 1918
- · - Front Line at 11 November 1918
—— National Boundaries
········ Army Boundaries (approximate)

0 10 20 30 40 50

MILES

Chapter 9

PEACE

TUESDAY 11 FEBRUARY 1919
29TH CASUALTY CLEARING STATION,
ROYAL ARMY MEDICAL CORPS,
BONN, GERMANY

The nature of the hospital's work was now entirely different. The requirement for emergency surgery was negligible and, although its principal function as a CCS remained the same – to provide primary treatment and evacuation of patients to base – the hospital now also took on a peacetime role more akin to that of a regional health centre where minor injuries were treated and short-term patients often released back to their units without the need to be sent up the line.

The hospital was located in a vast, late nineteenth-century gothic building which had been a civil hospital before the war, taken over by the German Army as a military hospital in 1914, and now in the hands of the Allies. It was situated on a hill with amazing views over the city and the River Rhine.

During its first month of operation at Bonn, 29CCS admitted 644 patients, including Indians, Russians, Serbs and several British civilians. There were no more admissions of German soldiers or civilians as they were now the responsibility of the German authorities. There were twenty deaths in the hospital during the first month, several as a result of influenza which was rife in Germany. It was also a big change for personnel, after living and working for years under canvas, to be operating from a spacious building with plenty of accommodation for patients and staff alike.

The official peace treaty between Germany and the European Allies, the Treaty of Versailles, was not signed until 28 June 1919 and during the seven month period from the Armistice to its signing, the blockade of Germany was maintained by the Allies. Consequently, there were serious food shortages among the civilian population and it is estimated that, during this interim period, around a quarter of a million German civilians died from disease and starvation – roughly half the number that had died during the war itself. The Colonel wrote:

> It is disturbing to see the degree of suffering around us. There are acute shortages of food and medical supplies but there are strict rules forbidding fraternisation and we are not allowed to help in any way. It is true that the Germans brought this upon themselves, but these are women, children and old men who had little say in events. As is so often the case, the innocent and defenceless are left to pay the bill for the aspirations and recklessness of their leaders.

Members of the Army of Occupation were reminded that Germany and the Allies were still technically at war and, in the event of their failing to ratify the treaty, there would be no alternative to a resumption of the fighting, which would inevitably result in a total occupation of Germany.

However, Britain's massive citizen army had signed on for hostilities only or were Territorial Army soldiers and, with Germany clearly defeated and the Allied forces reasonably well established in commanding positions, it was time to start releasing some of the temporary officers, men and nursing sisters. The extent of the wartime augmentation within the AMS can be seen in the table below:

ARMY MEDICAL SERVICES PERSONNEL

	OFFICERS	SOLDIERS	SISTERS	TOTAL
1914	900	9,000	300	10,200
1918	13,000	154,000	10,404	177,404

Little groups of two or three men, their kit packed and awaiting transport to Cologne for demobilization, became a common sight. Their loss was keenly felt, as many of them, after several years' service in France, were seasoned and very competent members of the team. A particular loss to the Colonel was on 13 February when RSM Charlesworth and Quartermaster Sergeant (QMS) Clarke left together for demobilisation; they were both key personnel within the unit.

On 16 March, and with a view to improving the standard of catering, Pte Knibbs and Pte Sutherland were posted to the Second Army School of Cooking in Cologne for a four-week course. With acute shortages of food among the civilian population, prostitution was rampant, with a resultant surge in venereal diseases among the troops. On 18 March the CO assembled the whole unit for a lecture on the subject.

Throughout the spring and summer the demobs continued, the strength being balanced, to some extent, by groups of soldiers from the infantry volunteering for transfer to the RAMC. Later, men would be transferred compulsorily; on one such occasion, 29CCS received a draft of twenty men from the Manchester Regiment, Bedfordshire Regiment, Royal West Kent Regiment and Lancashire Fusiliers. With the compulsory drafts, several men were usually returned to their units as 'unsuitable for service in RAMC'.

On 11 May the hospital was inspected by the commander-in-chief of the new British Army of the Rhine, Gen. Sir William Robertson*. 'Wully' Robertson, as Chief of the Imperial General Staff (CIGS) from 1915 to 1918, had been Haig's key ally in the battle against Lloyd George's parsimony prior to the German March Offensive. He had resigned his post in February 1918 amidst much acrimony. He must have been impressed by what he saw at 29CCS as on 8 June as Lt Col Carmichael was awarded the Order of the British Empire (OBE).

High summer came and the routine of the hospital settled into warm weather mode. As a permanent, smooth-running, military establishment with plenty of spare accommodation, 29CCS became the mother unit for several soldiers from other regiments and corps who messed with the hospital while attending courses in Cologne.

---

* Later field marshal, Robertson was the first man in the British Army to rise from the rank of private to field marshal.

On 16 August four soldiers of No.12 Graves Registration Unit joined on attachment to the unit. With the massive number of British and Commonwealth soldiers who had lost their lives in France and Belgium, the recovery of human remains, consolidation of hundreds of temporary burial sites, the marking and registration of graves and collection of details of the many thousands of soldiers whose remains were not recovered presented an awesome task.

It had been started in the first year of the war when a 45-year-old Englishman, Fabian Ware, in charge of a British Red Cross Mobile Unit, had recognised the importance of arrangements to ensure that every soldier's death was recorded and his grave, if one existed, properly cared for. Ware's Red Cross Unit compiled details of every grave they came across and in 1915 its work was recognised by the government with the change of its medical role to one solely concerned with war graves. The unit was incorporated into the Army and became the Graves Registration Commission.

The commander-in-chief, Gen. Haig, reported to the War Office on the work of the commission:

> It is fully recognised that the work of the organisation is of purely sentimental value, and that it does not directly contribute to the successful termination of the war. It has, however, an extraordinary moral value to the troops in the field as well as to the relatives and friends of the dead at home. The mere fact that these officers visit day after day the cemeteries close behind the trenches, fully exposed to shell and rifle fire, accurately to record not only the names of the dead, but also the exact place of burial, has a symbolic value to the men which it would be difficult to exaggerate. Further, it should be borne in mind that on the termination of hostilities the Nation will demand an account from the government as to the steps which have been taken to mark and classify the burial places of the dead, steps which can only be effectively taken at, or soon after, burial.

Closely supported by the Prince of Wales, Ware developed the commission's activities and in 1917 presented a paper to the Imperial War Conference, which resulted in the establishment by Royal Charter of the Imperial War Graves Commission (IWGC). For the remainder of the war, the commission's Graves Registration Units worked ceaselessly to keep pace with the ever-growing number of casualties. The larger Allied burial grounds tended to be adjacent to the field hospitals and were, by and large, well documented by the RAMC staff. Small sections of the Graves Registration Units were therefore attached to field ambulances and casualty clearing stations, but much of the work was done by mobile sections who built up local intelligence networks of priests and other French civilians, COs of units in the area, staff of Regimental Aid Posts and Advanced Dressing Stations who kept them informed of the exact location of every skirmish and known fatality. The GR teams would comb the devastated battlefields to search out and identify the dead, and to map and record the thousands of small frontline burial grounds.

At the end of hostilities the work of the commission was only just starting. The frontline burial grounds had to be consolidated with the large cemeteries being established on ground granted to Britain in perpetuity by the French and Belgian governments. These cemeteries were to be designed and constructed to the finest specifications. The country's leading architects were invited to submit proposals which would be fitting tributes to the fallen. Thousands of men were recruited to undertake the clearance and construction of the sites and stonemasons throughout Britain were commissioned to start carving the half-million headstones required.

At the same time the principles of the Imperial War Graves Commission were established and made known: the fundamental precept was one of complete equality between the graves and memorials, recognising the fact that the sacrifice of the most humble private soldier was every bit as great as that of his senior officers and that his remains were worthy of exactly the same degree of honour and respect.

The first principle was therefore that no body should be repatriated. All the fallen should be buried together on their old battlefields, side by side, as they had fought, in ground which, thanks to the generosity of the host nations, was British soil. Every known grave was to be marked with a headstone of uniform design, which would be permanent and engraved with the name, rank and number of the victim, together with the badge of his regiment or service. The families were invited to add a short personal quotation if they wished. No distinction was to be made on account of military or civil rank, wealth, race or creed.

BRITISH & COMMONWEALTH WAR DEAD

	IDENTIFIED	COMMEMORATED ON MEMORIAL	TOTAL
UK & Colonies	477,507	409,432	886,939
India *	8,054	66,133	74,187
Canada	45,507	19,469	64,976
Australia	38,608	23,358	61,966
New Zealand	11,761	6,291	18,052
South Africa	6,646	2,831	9,477
TOTAL	588,083	527,514	1,115,597

* Including what is today India, Pakistan and Bangladesh.

Normally speaking, British dead who had been buried in civilian cemeteries close to where they had fallen were moved after the war into large British IWGC cemeteries where they could lie beside their comrades and where their grave would be tended for all time by British gardeners. The exception to this was if the victim's religion forbade exhumation.

Anyone who has seen the extreme beauty and peace of the British war cemeteries in France and Belgium can judge for themselves whether the Commonwealth War Graves Commission (CWGC), as it is now called, has succeeded in the massive task they were commissioned by the nation to undertake.

An inspection of 29CCS on 17 August by DMS Rhine Army was the prelude to an even more important event three days later. On Wednesday 20 August the hospital was inspected by the Army Council, including the Rt Hon. Mr Winston Churchill and Field Marshal Sir Henry Wilson CIGS:

I think they were pleased with what they saw. We had to 'borrow' some patients with minor ailments from another hospital to fill our beds – the Bigwigs like to see plenty of activity! Mr Churchill is an extremely impressive man. I am told that he has been one of the principal advocates for the supply of food aid to German civilians, which is very much to his credit. When the big enemy attack was launched in March last year, he was apparently in the trenches very close to our camp at Grevillers so he must have been driven back with the same ferocity as we were. He asked if I was related to the Colonel Carmichael whom he had known in the Malakand Expedition. I said yes, he was my father, and he made some very flattering remarks about how we had both done our jobs well! I felt very honoured to have been recognised by such a great man.

Sir Henry Wilson, as you will know, is from an Ascendancy family in the North and has been involved in the political wrangles surrounding the question of Irish Home Rule.* He lost an eye and was seriously wounded in Burma and has since walked with a limp.

The year 1919 may, in many ways, be regarded as the year in which the political and military strategies for the rest of the twentieth century were locked into place: though the Treaty of Versailles between Germany and the Allied Powers had been ratified, and treaties were signed with Austria and Bulgaria, it was also the year in which Adolf Hitler founded the National Socialist Workers' Party in Germany, Benito Mussolini formed the *Fascia di combattimento* in Italy and the Soviet Republic was established in Russia following the failure of Allied intervention to assist the White Russians against the Bolsheviks. The pieces were thus moved into place for the next round of total warfare.

In Northern France and Belgium, the vast military dominion which was the Allied Armies in Europe continued to disperse; its enormous stores and ammunition depots which were townships in themselves; the tented hospital cities; the immeasurable networks of trenches and tunnels with names like 'Piccadilly', 'Old Kent Road' and 'Sauchiehall Street'; the derelict tanks, wrecked aircraft, abandoned artillery pieces; the thousands of square miles of town and country reduced to a moonscape of desolation and destruction, and the remains of the millions of brave men from countries around the world who would never return to

---

* Three years later he was murdered on the doorstep of his London house by two IRA gunmen. They shot nine bullets into him as he struggled to draw his sword to defend himself, though his right arm had been shattered by the first shots.

their homelands. The battlefields of Picardy would never lose the scars of war completely but, bit by bit, year after year, the damage would have to be righted and the land returned to its agricultural origins.

In Germany, after a period of political chaos following the abdication of the Kaiser, the Weimar Republic came into being in February 1919, committed to a democratic system under which all adults above the age of 21 would elect members of the Reichstadt by proportional representation and the Reichstadt would appoint the government. After years of autocracy it was to be government of the people, voted for by the people. But the reparations demanded in the Treaty of Versailles were harsh and the new government's attempts at compliance were attacked by extremists from the left and the right; the communists wanted to emulate Russia in the formation of a totalitarian workers' state and the hardline nationalists refused to accept that Germany had been defeated, as the German Army had never surrendered. Signatories of the Armistice were branded as 'The November Criminals' and the nationalists advocated complete rejection of the Treaty of Versailles.

Hopes for the efficacy of proportional representation were soon destroyed by the realities of the system: the Reichstadt ground to an impotent halt, unable to pass any laws due to the in-fighting among the many small political groups which the system created.

The year 1919 saw riots and demonstrations from both ends of the political spectrum, which would eventually lead to the notorious hyperinflation of the Weimar Republic.

In July, DDMS X Corps warned Lt Col Carmichael that he should be prepared for a move in the autumn. After so many years of overseas service he hoped for a home appointment:

> ... but he said that with the shortage of regular officers in my rank, another overseas command would be probable. I certainly hope not but, if this is the case, I will get a good long period of embarkation leave which will give me time to help find a suitable house for you and the *butchas** and to see you settled in before I go ...
>
> We have the most beautiful view from the hospital out over Bonn and the River Rhine. Looking at the tranquility of the city at dusk,

---

* *Butchas* – Hindustani for children.

the twinkling lights and meandering columns of smoke from chimneys, it is difficult to remember the terrible violence of life less than a year ago. I am still completely stunned by the magnitude of the losses and suffering in this awful war. Thank God (and the Yanks) that we came out on top! To have endured such ghastly privation and sacrifice and to have finished up under the Kaiser's jackboot would have been intolerable. Thank God too for the character of the ordinary British Tommy whose courage and resilience has kept morale from foundering when things were looking really bad. I have learned so much about the British character in adversity and have gained an even greater respect for the soldiers for whom we care. To see, as I have many times, a ward full of men with appalling injuries, some blinded, some limbless and some with no chance of recovery, and invariably to find among them one or two who, despite the severity of their wounds, will be bantering with their chums, teasing the nurses and foreign patients and generally keeping spirits high, is to see the British at their very best.

I think it was Samuel Johnson who said that every man thinks meanly of himself for never having been a soldier or never having been to sea. There will be very few of these in Britain in the years ahead and one can only hope that the Nation will provide for those who have served their country with such diligence and courage. They will need jobs and decent houses and the thousands who are limbless or maimed in other ways will have earned a right to the finest medical care we can provide.

On 13 October 1919 Lt Col Carmichael received orders to proceed to the UK for eight weeks' leave prior to sailing for Egypt to take command of No.166 Combined Field Ambulance.

His replacement was to be Lt Col O.W.A. Elsner OBE, DSO, RAMC, another Irishman, who could not take command until the 29th, so the following day he handed over temporary command of 29CCS to his second-in-command, Maj. R.B. Roe RAMC, and left Germany for the UK.

Chapter 10

EPILOGUE

Reverting to his sustantive rank, Maj. Carmichael sailed from Southampton on 11 December 1919 and on the 21st took over command of No.166 Combined Field Ambulance near Alexandria. He was there for one year and one month before being moved to command the Ras-el-Tin Military Hospital, and was then appointed senior MO Alexandria.

Returning to the UK, he took command of Hounslow Military Hospital on Christmas Day 1921, before being posted abroad to Constantinople in September 1922, returning a year later to take his promotion exam in Aldershot, which he passed with distinction. He was also delighted to learn that his son, Donald, despite the late start to his secondary education, had passed well into Sandhurst.

His uncle, Col William Ferris, who had been Governor of Aden and of British Somaliland, wrote on 30 December 1923 to congratulate him on both achievements:

I just write a line to congratulate you on the success of Donald in passing into Sandhurst. It seems to me to do him infinite credit getting through at the first try and I wonder under the circumstances if it would be worthwhile to run him for Woolwich. Gunners and Sappers seem in these days to be the only branches of the Service that are likely to give a lad a career and Donald with his interest in mechanics should make a good Sapper. Otherwise consider putting him into the Tanks as these are the weapons which are going to dominate the battlefields of the future. I must congratulate you too in getting satisfactorily through your promotion exam – I don't know how you managed it considering the way you have been bucketed about during the last two years. It must be a great load off your mind and if those of your Service who are members of my Club are to be believed, there is likely to be a run of promotion soon. I hope you managed to get leave to spend Xmas with your family, it was eminently a day for family parties to foregather over a common fire for it was a poisonous day outside and too gloomy for one to sit at home alone.

James Carmichael retired from the Army as a lieutenant colonel on 11 August 1925 and bought a private medical practice in Ewell, Surrey, and the following month his son, Donald, was commissioned as a second lieutenant in the Royal Tank Corps. His brother, Donald, had also retired from the Army and bought a practice in Putney; so the two brothers and two sisters, whose service lives had been on opposite sides of the world, were only a stone's throw from each other in later life.

James practised in Ewell for twelve years, during which he was also honorary physician at the Epsom and Ewell Hospital where the nurses recognised his military step as he came down the corridor and affectionately named him 'The General'. In 1937 he was diagnosed with stomach cancer. He sold his practice in Ewell and died on 22 July 1938. Hilda, his widow, lived to the age of 101 and was an honoured guest at the Golden Jubilee celebrations of the RAMC, in the presence of Her Majesty Queen Elizabeth, on 23 June 1948. Their son Donald had a full career in the Army retiring as a colonel.

The site of 29CCS in March 1918 is easy to find. Two fields, one opposite the other on either side of the D29 leading north-east-wards out of the village of Grévillers is where 29CCS and 3CCS were encamped when the Germans attacked in March 1918. Crops are now grown on both sides and the odd Charolais cow and calf graze where the great tented hospitals once stood. The old railway line on which so many thousands of wounded British soldiers were evacuated is still there, unused for many years and overgrown with weed and brambles. There is no sign of the spur running to the hospitals and on to the village, which was removed many years ago, and no sign of its junction with the main line.

Standing beside the railway track today and looking across the ground where the rows of marquees and bell tents stood, one can relive those awful two days in March 1918 when, with enemy shells passing overhead and bursting around them, both hospitals struggled to keep pace with the endless columns of grievously wounded men arriving throughout the day and night. One can readily picture the rows of stretchers lying on the ground beside the railway track, when all wards in the hospitals were full to overflowing and the ambulance trains could not arrive fast enough to keep pace with the casualties. And then the scramble to strike camp and evacuate as much of the stores and equipment as could be loaded before the German infantry arrived.

Grévillers British Cemetery is just before the old hospital site on the left-hand side of the road coming from the village. Some 2,100 Commonwealth soldiers are either buried or commemorated in this little patch of Britain. The New Zealand Division retook Grévillers during the Allied advance in August and were much involved in the fighting in this area. A handsome memorial to 450 of its officers and men with no known grave is at the far end of the cemetery, one of seven in France and Belgium erected to the memory of the brave New Zealanders.

Dernancourt, or Edgehill as the British knew it, a village just outside Albert, had been a hospital site throughout the war and became the hub of Allied medical activity during the March 1918 retreat. At one point there were five CCSs here, all of which had to be evacuated in a hurry ahead of the German advance. The last to leave was 29CCS, whose departure was continually delayed by bombing from enemy aircraft. The Dernancourt Communal Cemetery Extension is about the same size as the Grévillers Cemetery, with around 2,100 burials and commemorations, 425 of which are of Australian soldiers, many brought in after the war in the process of consolidation of several small battlefield burial grounds.

The village has particular links with Australia as there was always an Australian CCS here while the village was in Allied hands, and it was a well remembered rest area for Australian troops back from the frontline. After the war the village was 'adopted' by the people of South Australia who generously provided much of the funds needed to restore it to normality in the 1920s. Reminders of the link can be seen today with the 'Rue d'Australie' and the 'Adelaide Hall'.

The route taken by 29CCS on its march from Dernancourt to Gézaincourt is mainly across flat agricultural land that has changed little since 1918. A 22-mile march, in the middle of the night, by hungry men who had worked flat out for four days and had had no more than a couple of hours sleep at a time, was a remarkable feat of endurance. The French hospice in Warloy-Baillon, where the officers snatched three hours sleep on the floor of the porter's lodge, is now a retirement home; the barn in which the men slept is the laundry for the home. There is no trace of the airfield where the Colonel begged a bath and a shave from one of the young pilots.

Gézaincourt is a quiet village just south-west of Doullens and the hospital site is a little farther on at the Bagneux British Military Cemetery. It is signposted and accessible, with care, up a very rough, potholed track. The railway, now disused and overgrown, runs along the cemetery's north-west boundary and the casualty clearing stations were sited in the long, green valley, now under cultivation, below the cemetery. The nearby chateau housed the Gézaincourt Officers' Hospital, which was run by the staff of one or other of the CCSs at Bagneux. The sisters from the hospitals slept on the top floor of the chateau, though their mess tent was in the main hospital compound. Apart from the bombing of the Canadian hospital at Doullens, this area was always behind the frontline and avoided the devastation suffered by towns and villages further to the east. This is reflected in the quiet and peaceful ambience of the Bagneux cemetery today. Being isolated, with a rough approach and away from the main pilgrimage circuit, it receives few visitors, yet is as beautiful and meticulously cared for as the best known and most frequently visited CWGC cemeteries. Here among professionally pruned English roses and green, meticulously tended turf, lie the remains of 1,374 British and Commonwealth men and women. They are the usual wide assortment of ages, ranks, nationalities and units: here are men from the Royal Navy, the Army and the recently formed RAF; from Britain, Canada, Australia, New Zealand and China; from experienced senior soldiers in their 40s to callow youths who had not started shaving; from private soldiers to a battalion and a divisional commander.

Here, together, are the graves of the thirteen Canadian doctors, nurses and orderlies who were killed when the operating theatre in No.3 Canadian Stationary Hospital in the Citadelle at Doullens received a direct hit from a German bomb on 27 May 1918; here also lie the remains of Lt Col Hugh Courtenay DSO, MC, the gallant 30-year-old commander of the 1st Bedfordshire Regiment, who with seven of his officers was killed in the attack on Achiet-le-Grand on 23 August 1918; and of Brig. Gen. Lumley Owen William Jones DSO, aged 40, who played cricket for Winchester and was, on 3 September 1918, the last of twelve British general officers to be killed on the Somme; and of Hien Ting Linn, one of two Chinese coolies of the 95,000 strong Chinese Labour Corps which gave hard and loyal service in France throughout the war; their graves, with respect to their beliefs, are set aside from the main Christian burial area, their headstones of the standard pattern bearing their names engraved in Chinese by Chinese masons and including in English the words: 'A good reputation endures for ever'. And here, among hundreds like him, lie the remains of Pte John William Lawrenson of the 15th Durham Light Infantry, who was mortally wounded in the intensive fighting in August 1918 and was one of fifteen soldiers to die in 29CCS on 27 August. He, like many here, is still mourned by his descendants who, during a recent pilgrimage to his grave, left a photograph of him with the visitors' book at the cemetery – a young man proud in his khaki uniform and mercifully unaware of how little of his life remained.

Unlike Gézaincourt, Delsaux Farm, near Beugny, had been the scene of heavy fighting in all phases of the Somme battles right up to 2 September 1918 when it was finally retaken by the advancing 5th Division. 29CCS arrived here on 31 September and much clearance and levelling of the shell-blasted ground was necessary before hospital tents could be pitched and the burial ground, which had been started by the Germans after they retook the site in March 1918, put back into service and extended. The frontline trenches of the German Beugny–Ytres Defensive Line actually ran across the corner of the present day cemetery, so the great Cross of Sacrifice and the first two rows of graves in Plot 1 stand above a spot where steel-helmeted German soldiers once crouched over their machine guns awaiting the next wave of British Tommies to climb from their trenches and launch themselves into the lethal rush across no man's land.

At Delsaux Farm, in the last six weeks of the war, 29CCS dealt with the aftermath of some of the fiercest fighting in the entire campaign. Casualties were massive during the big Allied attacks. Admission figures were horrific: 8 October (644); 25 October (657); 5 November, six days before the Armistice, (406). There is no trace today of the railway which ran alongside the road on the opposite side to the farm, but one can picture the continuous convoys of ambulances and requisitioned buses arriving throughout the day and night from Caudry, after a long journey along shell-cratered roads, and disgorging their cargoes of dying and hideously wounded men whose condition had almost certainly deteriorated after their bumpy ride.

On a rainy day it is also easy to picture the rows of hospital tents in the fields beyond the railway after several days of continuous rain, the canvas sodden and sagging; the guy ropes straining and dripping water; the ditches overflowing and men in their green waterproof gas capes with shovels and buckets working frantically to clear the drains before the duckboarded paths between the tents became flooded. Christmas 1918 must certainly have lacked some of its traditional sparkle for the men of 29CCS.

Their new quarters in Bonn after life under canvas at Delsaux Farm, followed by sixteen days living in freezing railway boxcars, must have seemed the height of luxury. The St Marien Hospital had been built as a civilian hospital in the late nineteenth century and had been taken over by the German Army as a military hospital during the war.

When the Canadians moved into Bonn at the end of hostilities, they examined premises all over the town for suitability as their main hospital. St Marien's was clearly the best, but the Germans were very reluctant to hand it over and tried, by every means in their power, to block the Canadians' acquisition. The Canadians persisted with their demands and ultimately prevailed. Though they had to post two officers in the hospital during the handover period to stop the Germans from removing equipment and furniture which they were meant to leave behind. By the end of the year 1CCS (Canadian), were, in the words of their CO: '... snuggly seated in the best hospital in Bonn'.

After successive occupations by Canadian, British and French medical units, St Marien's was handed back to Germany in the 1920s and is still used as a hospital today, though the handsome old building is now the centre of a huge hospital complex, surrounded by modern blocks and unrecognisable in its original form.

When 29CCS were here they buried their dead in the German cemetery on Kolnstrasse. In the 1920s it was decided to consolidate several British burial grounds throughout Germany into four main cemeteries, one of which was the Cologne South Cemetery which already contained the graves of some 1,000 British prisoners buried there by the Germans during the war. All the burials from 29CCS in the Kolnstrasse, Bonn, were therefore moved to Cologne South, except for the remains of three Indian artillerymen, Driver (Dvr) Keso Singh and Dvr Panna Singh, and Gnr Phul Singh of the Royal Horse and Field Artillery of the Indian Army, who died in 1919 and whose religion forbade the exhumation of their graves. Their bodies lie in honour in a little plot near the north corner of the north cemetery in the huge civilian and German military burial grounds on Kolnstrasse, Bonn.

Of the many military hospitals in the UK in which James Carmichael served during his career, not one remains today. Hounslow Military Hospital or 'Percy House', originally a school in the town workhouse, was demolished in 1978; the First World War Military Hospital in Crowborough or 'Harecombe Manor' is now a nursing home; Queen Alexandra's Military Hospital, Millbank, closed in the 1970s and is now part of Tate Britain; The Royal Army Medical College is today the Chelsea College of Art and Design; The Royal Victoria Hospital, Netley, was demolished in 1966 except for the chapel, which still stands in what is now the Royal Victoria Country Park.

Indeed, all of the great British Military Hospitals, with their reputation for excellence, have now disappeared. The most modern and state-of-the-art service hospital, the Queen Elizabeth Military Hospital in Woolwich, closed in 1995 and became a civilian hospital. Haslar Royal Naval, and latterly joint-service, Hospital at Gosport was the last service hospital to close in 2009. Today, British servicemen wounded in action receive superb first-line attention in field hospitals manned by Army doctors, nurses and orderlies, many of them Territorials. For ongoing care they are then taken to a special ward in a civilian hospital where they must rely for their treatment on the already overburdened National Health Service.

The last word shall be left to Lt Col J.C.G. Carmichael in a letter from Constantinople, where he was serving in August 1923, to his son Donald who was about to start his military career at Sandhurst:

It is difficult to assimilate the full horror of the late war, the devastation it has spread through the countryside and towns of Europe, the tragedy and desperation it has inflicted on millions of mothers, wives and daughters, the lives of the tens of millions of young men of all nations it has cut short, and the horrific injuries and disabilities it has imposed on millions of others. Nothing in my medical training and experience prepared me for the horrific and heartbreaking sights and sounds I witnessed daily during the last two bloody years of the conflict.

I mention this to you as my overwhelming resolution, and that of all who have lived through this cataclysmic event, must be that it must never, never be allowed to happen again. All the powers of diplomacy of the civilised world must be directed to this end and we must reconcile ourselves to whatever public expenditure is necessary to maintain our Army and Navy at levels which will deter, or can immediately suppress, any future attempt, by any nation, to subject humanity to a similar outrage.

The profession you have chosen is an honourable one, and one which our family has followed for two hundred years, but more importantly, it is the only profession which can ensure that the follies of the past are not repeated. We must remain strong if we wish to remain free. Superior military strength, and the political resolve to use it where necessary, is the only thing which will intimidate the international bullies and ensure the peace of the world.

In 1940, two years after his death, the British Empire was again at war with Germany.

A visit to Gézaincourt British War Cemetery at Bagneux

A rough lane leads across a blood-red track
Which leads away around a curve.
Its wooden sleepers disintegrating with time.
No train, no sign of steam and smoke
Nor engine whistle echoing across the gorge.
Both long gone. Yet in the far and distant past
A century ago, here stood a hospital
Where doctors laboured night and day,
And soldiers cried from injuries received
On these fair fields of distant France.
Here trains arrived with squeal of brakes,
Doors opened, shut and spilt out living souls,
And the dead!
For some, this was a final end,
With no family to come and mourn
And shed tears of grief at funerals,
Just buried here with simple wooden cross.
Young men with so much life to live.

A friend now kneels this day before the place
Where a kinsman finally rests.
The only visitor since World War One.
He pays humble honour to the man
He never knew. A fading khaki photograph.
He ponders. Alive when this was shot.
He leaves some flowers and a note,
Simple, silent symbols of respect.
He slowly rises from his knees;
And stands transfixed in the quietness
In this corner of a foreign field,
Drinking in the saddened beauty of this hour.
Then from high above this steep-side vale
There bursts the bud and birdsong of the spring.
He ponders, what may have been.
Forgotten hope.
That lingers even now as memories in his mind.

David Holme

APPENDIX A

THE BRITISH ARMY MEDICAL ESTABLISHMENT ON THE WESTERN FRONT

A look at the vast medical support network required to sustain the Army in France and Belgium gives some idea of the enormity of the Military Operation.

GENERAL HOSPITALS

No.1 General Hospital	Taken over by No.2 (Presbyterian) USA Base Hospital, July 1917
No.2 General Hospital	
No.3 General Hospital	
No.4 General Hospital	
No.5 General Hospital	
No.6 General Hospital	
No.7 General Hospital	Abandoned at Amiens during Retreat from Mons. Reformed at Malassise June 1915
No.8 General Hospital	
No.9 General Hospital	Taken over by No.4 (Cleveland) USA Base Hospital, July 1917
No.10 General Hospital	
No.11 General Hospital	Taken over by No.5 (Harvard) USA Base Hospital, July 1917. Moved to Italy 15 November 1917.

	US Personnel transferred to No.13 General Hospital
No.12 General Hospital	Taken over by No.21 (St. Louis) USA Base Hospital, July 1917
No.13 General Hospital	Taken over by No.5 (Harvard) USA Base Hospital. Personnel previously with No.11 General Hospital
No.14 General Hospital	
No.16 General Hospital	Taken over by No.10 (Philadelphia) USA Base Hospital, June 1917
No.18 General Hospital	Taken over by No.12 (Chicago) USA Base Hospital, July 1917
No. 20 General Hospital	
No.22 General Hospital	Staffed by Harvard Voluntary Medical Unit
No.23 General Hospital	Staffed by Chicago Voluntary Medical Unit July 1915. Taken over by No.7 Canadian General Hospital, November 1916
No.24 General Hospital	
No.25 General Hospital	
No.26 General Hospital	
No.30 General Hospital	Previously at Palermo
No.35 General Hospital	Previously Lahore British General Hospital
No.39 General Hospital	Previously No.9 Stationary Hospital
No. 47 General Hospital	
No.51 General Hospital	
No.53 (London) General Hospital	Territorial Force Unit
No.54 (London) General Hospital	Territorial Force Unit
No.55 (Eastern) General Hospital	Territorial Force Unit
No.56 (Southern) General Hospital	Territorial Force Unit
No.57 (Western) General Hospital	Territorial Force Unit
No.58 (Scottish) General Hospital	Territorial Force Unit
No.59 (Northern) General Hospital	Territorial Force Unit
No.72 General Hospital	
No.73 General Hospital	
No.74 General Hospital	
No.81 General Hospital	Previously in Malta
No.83 General Hospital	Previously No.13 Stationary Hospital
No.1 Canadian General Hospital	Arrived England from Canada October 1914
No.2 Canadian General Hospital	Arrived England from Canada October 1914

No.3 Canadian General Hospital	Arrived England from Canada May 1915
No.6 Canadian General Hospital	
No.7 Canadian General Hospital	Previously in Egypt. Took over No.23. British General Hospital November 1916
No.8 Canadian General Hospital	Previously No.1 Canadian Stationary Hospital
No.1 Australian General Hospital	Previously in Egypt
No.2 Australian General Hospital	Previously in Egypt
No.3 Australian General Hospital	Previously at Brighton
No.1 South African General Hospital	
Lahore Indian General Hospital	
Meerut Indian General Hospital	Left for Mesopotamia December 1915
Secunderabad Indian General Hospital	Left for Mesopotamia December 1915
Lahore British General Hospital	Became No.35 General Hospital May 1916
Meerut British General Hospital	Became No.25 General Hospital May 1916
Rawalpindi British General Hospital	Left for Mesopotamia December 1915

STATIONARY HOSPITALS

No.1 Stationary Hospital	
No.2 Stationary Hospital	
No.3 Stationary Hospital	
No.4 Stationary Hospital	
No.5 Stationary Hospital	
No.6 Stationary Hospital	
No.7 Stationary Hospital	
No.8 Stationary Hospital	
No.9 Stationary Hospital	Became No.39 General Hospital June 1916
No.10 Stationary Hospital	
No.11 Stationary Hospital	
No.12 Stationary Hospital	
No.13 Stationary Hospital	Became No.83 General Hospital May 1917
No.14 Stationary Hospital	
No.25 Stationary Hospital	Previously Meerut British General Hospital

No.27 Stationary Hospital	Havre Isolation Hospital. Became part of No.2 General Hospital May 1916
No.28 Stationary Hospital	Etaples Isolation Hospital. Became Isolation Block of No.24 General Hospital May 1916 then No.46 Stationary Hospital April 1917
No.32 Stationary Hospital	Previously Australian Voluntary Hospital
No.38 Stationary Hospital	Moved to Italy November 1917
No.39 Stationary Hospital	
No.40 Stationary Hospital	
No.41 Stationary Hospital	
No.42 Stationary Hospital	
No.46 Stationary Hospital	Previously Isolation Block No.24 Stationary Hospital
No.52 Stationary Hospital	Previously part of No.2 General Hospital
Stationary Hospital Abancourt	
Stationary Hospital Marseilles	Previously part of No.39 General Hospital and No.2 Australian General Hospital
Station Hospital Paris	
No.1 Canadian Stationary Hospital	Moved to Salonika July 1915
No.2 Canadian Stationary Hospital	
No.3 Canadian Stationary Hospital	Previously in Egypt
No.4 Canadian Stationary Hospital	Became No.8 Canadian General Hospital July 1916
No.5 Canadian Stationary Hospital	Previously in Egypt and No.7 Canadian General Hospital
No.7 Canadian Stationary Hospital	
No.8 Canadian Stationary Hospital	Moved to England May 1916
No.9 Canadian Stationary Hospital	
No.10 Canadian Stationary Hospital	
New Zealand Stationary Hospital	Previously in Egypt
Meerut Stationary Hospital	Moved to Mesopotamia December 1915
Lahore Stationary Hospital	Moved to Mesopotamia March 1916

VOLUNTARY HOSPITALS

No.1 Red Cross Hospital, Le Touquet	Duchess of Westminster's Hospital
No.2 Red Cross Hospital, Rouen	

No. 3 Red Cross Hospital, Abbeville	Friends' Ambulance Unit
No. 4 Red Cross Hospital, Wimereux	Sir Henry Norman's Hospital
No. 5 Red Cross Hospital, Wimereux	Lady Hadfield's Anglo-American Hospital
No. 6 Red Cross Hospital, Etaples	Liverpool Merchants' Hospital
No. 7 Red Cross Hospital, Boulogne & Etaples	Allied Forces Base Hospital
No. 8 Red Cross Hospital, Calais & Paris Plage	Baltic & Corn Exchange Hospital
No. 9 Red Cross Hospital,	Millicent Duchess of Sutherland's Dunkirk & Calais Hospital
No. 10 Red Cross Hospital, Le Tréport	Lady Murray's Hospital. Previously worked with French Red Cross
Australian Voluntary Aid Hospital	Became No. 32 Stationary Hospital, St. Nazaire & Wimereux
St John Ambulance Brigade Hospital, Etaples	
Scottish Red Cross Mobile Unit, Rouen	Attached to No. 11 Stationary Hospital
Queen Alexandra Hospital, Dunkirk	Friends' Ambulance Unit
Malassise Hospital (British Red Cross)	Taken over by No. 7 Gen Hospital 1915

CONVALESCENT DEPOTS

No. 1 Convalescent Depot	
No. 2 Convalescent Depot	
No. 3 Convalescent Depot	
No. 4 Convalescent Depot	
No. 5 Convalescent Depot	
No. 6 Convalescent Depot	
No. 7 Convalescent Depot	
No. 8 Convalescent Home for Officers	Michelham Convalescent Home
No. 10 Convalescent Depot	
No. 11 Convalescent Depot	
No. 12 Convalescent Depot	
No. 13 Convalescent Depot	
No. 14 Convalescent Depot	
No. 15 Convalescent Depot	Became a POW Camp
No. 16 Convalescent Depot	
No. 8 Indian Convalescent Depot	Closed December 1915
No. 9 Indian Convalescent Depot	
Indian Convalescent Depot, Rouen	Closed April 1915

MEDICAL STORES BASE DEPOTS

No.1 Base Depot Medical Stores	
No.2 Base Depot Medical Stores	
No.3 Base Depot Medical Stores	
No.6 Base Depot Medical Stores	
No.13 Base Depot Medical Stores	

MEDICAL STORES ADVANCED DEPOTS

No.1 Advanced Depot Medical Stores	
No.2 Advanced Depot Medical Stores	
No.3 Advanced Depot Medical Stores	
No.11 Advanced Depot Medical Stores	
No.12 Advanced Depot Medical Stores	
No.13 Advanced Depot Medical Stores	
No.14 Advanced Depot Medical Stores	
No.15 Advanced Depot Medical Stores	
No.16 Advanced Depot Medical Stores	
No.17 Advanced Depot Medical Stores	Captured by Germans at Mont Notre Dame, March 1918
No.18 Advanced Depot Medical Stores	
No.19 Advanced Depot Medical Stores	
No.31 Advanced Depot Medical Stores	
No.32 Advanced Depot Medical Stores	Moved to Italy November 1917
No.33 Advanced Depot Medical Stores	
No.34 Advanced Depot Medical Stores	
No.13 Advanced Depot Medical Stores	Formed December 1919 in Germany
No.2 Canadian Advanced Depot Medical Stores	

SANITARY SECTIONS

No.1 Sanitary Section	
No.2 Sanitary Section	
No.3a Sanitary Section	
No.4 Sanitary Section	Moved to Italy November 1917
No.4a Sanitary Section	
No.5a Sanitary Section	
No.6 Sanitary Section	

No.7 Sanitary Section	Moved to Salonika January 1916
No.8 Sanitary Section	
No.9 Sanitary Section	
No.10 Sanitary Section	
No.11 Sanitary Section	
No.12 Sanitary Section	
No.13 Sanitary Section	
No.14 Sanitary Section	Moved to Italy November 1917
No.16 Sanitary Section	Previously in Egypt
No.17 Sanitary Section	
No.20 Sanitary Section	
No.21 Sanitary Section	Previously in Egypt
No.22 Sanitary Section	Previously in Egypt
No.23 Sanitary Section	
No.25 Sanitary Section	
No.27 Sanitary Section	
No.32 Sanitary Section	
No.33 Sanitary Section	
No.34 Sanitary Section	
No.35 Sanitary Section	
No.36 Sanitary Section	Moved to Italy December 1917
No.37 Sanitary Section	Absorbed into No.87 San Sect February 1919
No.38 Sanitary Section	
No.39 Sanitary Section	Moved to Salonika November 1915
No.40 Sanitary Section	
No.41 Sanitary Section	
No.42 Sanitary Section	
No.44 Sanitary Section	
No.45 Sanitary Section	
47th (London) Divisional Sanitary Section	
48th (S. Midland) Divisional Sanitary Section	
49th (W. Riding) Divisional Sanitary Section	
50th (Northumbrian) Divisional Sanitary Section	
51st (Highland) Division Sanitary Section	
52nd Divisional Sanitary Section	Previously in Egypt
55th Divisional Sanitary Section	
56th Divisional Sanitary Section	
57th Divisional Sanitary Section	
58th Divisional Sanitary Section	
59th Divisional Sanitary Section	
60th Divisional Sanitary Section	Moved to Salonika December 1916
61st Divisional Sanitary Section	

62nd Divisional Sanitary Section	
63rd Divisional Sanitary Section	
66th (E. Lancs) Division San Section	
No.70 Sanitary Section	
No.71 Sanitary Section	Previously in Egypt
No.72 Sanitary Section	
No.73 Sanitary Section	Moved to Italy November 1917
No.74 Sanitary Section	
No.75 Sanitary Section	
No.76 Sanitary Section	
No.77 Sanitary Section	
No.81 Sanitary Section	
No.82 Sanitary Section	
No.83 Sanitary Section	
No.84 Sanitary Section	Moved to Italy November 1917
No.87 Sanitary Section	Previously in Italy
No.109 Sanitary Section	
No.111 Sanitary Section	
No.119 Sanitary Section	
No.120 Sanitary Section	
1st London Sanitary Section	
1st Canadian Divisional Sanitary Section	
2nd Canadian Divisional Sanitary Section	
4th Canadian Divisional Sanitary Section	
5th Canadian Sanitary Section	
1st Australian Sanitary Section	Previously in Egypt
2nd Australian Sanitary Section	Previously in Egypt
3rd Australian Sanitary Section	
4th Australian Sanitary Section	Previously in Egypt
5th Australian Sanitary Section	
1st NZ Divisional Sanitary Section	Previously in Egypt
1st Indian Cavalry Divisional Sanitary Section	Moved to Egypt March 1918
2nd Indian Cavalry Divisional Sanitary Section	Moved to Egypt March 1918
3rd Indian Cavalry Divisional Sanitary Section	Moved to Mesopotamia December 1915
No.4 Meerut Divisional Sanitary Section	Moved to Mesopotamia December 1915

MOBILE LABORATORIES

No.1 Mobile Bacteriological Laboratory	
No.2 Mobile Bacteriological Laboratory	
No.3 Mobile Bacteriological Laboratory	
No.4 Mobile Hygiene Laboratory	
No.5 Canadian Mobile Bacteriological Laboratory	
No.6 Mobile Hygiene Laboratory	Renumbered No.15 May 1916
No.7 Mobile Bacteriological Laboratory	Moved to Italy November 1917
No.8 Mobile Bacteriological Laboratory	
No.9 Mobile Hygiene Laboratory	
No.10 Mobile Bacteriological Laboratory	
No.11 Mobile Bacteriological Laboratory	
No.12 Mobile Hygiene Laboratory	
No.13 Mobile Bacteriological Laboratory	
No.14 Mobile Bacteriological Laboratory	Moved to Italy December 1917
No.38 Welsh Divisional Mobile Bact Lab	Renumbered No.21 January 1916
No.15 Mobile Hygiene Laboratory	Moved to Italy November 1917
No.16 Mobile Bacteriological Laboratory	
No.17 Mobile Bacteriological Laboratory	
No.19 Mobile Bacteriological Laboratory	
No.20 Mobile Bacteriological Laboratory	
No.21 Mobile Bacteriological Laboratory	Previously No.38 Welsh
No.22 Mobile Hygiene Laboratory	
No.23 Mobile Bacteriological Laboratory	Moved to Italy December 1917
No.33 Mobile Bacteriological Laboratory	
No.39 Mobile Bacteriological Laboratory	

MOBILE X-RAY LABORATORIES

No.1 Mobile X-Ray Laboratory	
No.2 (Cheltenham College) Mobile X-Ray Laboratory	Presented by Cheltenham College
No.3 Mobile X-Ray Laboratory	
No.4 Mobile X-Ray Laboratory	
No.5 Mobile X-Ray Laboratory	

MOBILE DENTAL UNITS

No.1 Mobile Dental Unit	
No.2 Mobile Dental Unit	

No.3 Mobile Dental Unit

No.4 Mobile Dental Unit

No.5 Mobile Dental Unit

CASUALTY CLEARING STATIONS

No.1 Casualty Clearing Station	
No.2 Casualty Clearing Station	
No.3 Casualty Clearing Station	
No.4 Casualty Clearing Station	
No.5 Casualty Clearing Station	
No.6 Casualty Clearing Station	
No.7 (1/1st West Riding) CCS	
No.8 Casualty Clearing Station	
No.9 Casualty Clearing Station	
No.10 Casualty Clearing Station	
No.11 Casualty Clearing Station	Previously in Egypt
No.12 Casualty Clearing Station	
No.13 Casualty Clearing Station	Previously in Egypt
No.15 Casualty Clearing Station	
No.17 Casualty Clearing Station	
No.18 Casualty Clearing Station	
No.19 Casualty Clearing Station	
No.20 Casualty Clearing Station	
No.21 Casualty Clearing Station	
No.22 Casualty Clearing Station	
No.23 Casualty Clearing Station	
No.24 Casualty Clearing Station	Moved to Italy November 1917
No.27 Casualty Clearing Station	Moved to Salonika November 1915
No.28 Casualty Clearing Station	Moved to Salonika November 1915
No.29 Casualty Clearing Station	
No.30 Casualty Clearing Station	
No.32 Casualty Clearing Station	
No.33 Casualty Clearing Station	
No.34 (W. Lancs) Casualty Clearing Station	
No.35 Casualty Clearing Station	Moved to Salonika December 1916
No.36 Casualty Clearing Station	
No.37 Casualty Clearing Station	Captured by enemy May 1918. Reformed June 1918
No.38 Casualty Clearing Station	
No.39 Casualty Clearing Station	Moved to Italy November 1917
No.40 Casualty Clearing Station (Ulster Division)	

No.41 Casualty Clearing Station (38th Welsh Division)	
No.42 Casualty Clearing Station	
No.43 Casualty Clearing Station	
No.44 Casualty Clearing Station	
No.45 Casualty Clearing Station	
No.46 Casualty Clearing Station (1/1st Wessex)	
No.47 Casualty Clearing Station (1/1st Home Counties)	
No.48 Casualty Clearing Station	
No.49 Casualty Clearing Station	
No.50 Casualty Clearing Station (1/1st Northumbrian)	
No.51 Casualty Clearing Station (1/1st Highland)	
No.53 Casualty Clearing Station (1/1st North Midland)	
No.54 Casualty Clearing Station (1/2nd London)	
No.55 Casualty Clearing Station (2/2nd London)	
No.56 Casualty Clearing Station (1/1st South Midland)	
No.57 Casualty Clearing Station (2/1st West Lancs)	
No.58 Casualty Clearing Station (2/1st West Riding)	
No.59 Casualty Clearing Station (2/1st North Midland)	
No.61 Casualty Clearing Station (2/1st South Midland)	
No.62 Casualty Clearing Station (2/1st Northumbrian)	
No.63 Casualty Clearing Station (1/1st London)	
No.64 Casualty Clearing Station (1/1st East Lancs)	
No.1 Canadian Casualty Clearing Station	
No.2 Canadian Casualty Clearing Station	
No.3 Canadian Casualty Clearing Station	
No.4 Canadian Casualty Clearing Station	
No.1 Australian Casualty Clearing Station	Previously in Egypt
No.2 Australian Casualty Clearing Station	
No.3 Australian Casualty Clearing Station	
Meerut Casualty Clearing Station (No.20)	Moved to Mesopotamia Nov 1915
Lahore Casualty Clearing Station (No.15)	Moved to Mesopotamia Dec 1915
Lucknow Casualty Clearing Station	Returned to India March 1919

FIELD AMBULANCES

1st Division
No.1 Field Ambulance
No.2 Field Ambulance
No.3 Field Ambulance Joined Guards Division Aug 1915

2nd Division

No.4 Field Ambulance	Joined Guards Division Aug 1915
No.5 Field Ambulance	
No.6 Field Ambulance	

3rd Division

No.7 Field Ambulance	
No.8 Field Ambulance	
No.9 Field Ambulance	Joined Guards Division Aug 1915

4th Division

No.10 Field Ambulance	
No.11 Field Ambulance	
No.12 Field Ambulance	

5th Division

No.13 Field Ambulance	
No.14 Field Ambulance	
No.15 Field Ambulance	

6th Division

No.16 Field Ambulance	
No.17 Field Ambulance	
No.18 Field Ambulance	
No.19 Field Ambulance	Temp Attachment to 6th Division. Subsequently with 8th, 2nd and 33rd divisions
No.20 Field Ambulance	

7th Division

No.21 Field Ambulance	Moved to Italy November 1917
No.22 Field Ambulance	Moved to Italy November 1917
No.23 Field Ambulance	Moved to Italy November 1917

8th Division

No.24 Field Ambulance	Territorial Force Field Ambulance 1/1st Wessex
No.25 Field Ambulance	Territorial Force Field Ambulance 1/2nd Wessex
No.26 Field Ambulance	Territorial Force Field Ambulance 1/3rd Wessex

9th Division	
No.27 Field Ambulance	
No.28 Field Ambulance	
No.29 Field Ambulance	Replaced by No.1 South African Field Ambulance May 1916, which was relieved by No.76 Field Ambulance Sep 1918. No.29 Field Ambulance disbanded Feb 1917

11th Division	
No.33 Field Ambulance	Previously in Egypt
No.34 Field Ambulance	Previously in Egypt
No.35 Field Ambulance	Previously in Egypt

12th Division	
No.36 Field Ambulance	
No.37 Field Ambulance	
No.38 Field Ambulance	

14th Division	
No.42 Field Ambulance	
No.43 Field Ambulance	
No.44 Field Ambulance	

15th Division	
No.45 Field Ambulance	
No.46 Field Ambulance	
No.47 Field Ambulance	

37th Division	
No.48 Field Ambulance	
No.49 Field Ambulance	
No.50 Field Ambulance	

17th Division	
No.51 Field Ambulance	
No.52 Field Ambulance	
No.53 Field Ambulance	

18th Division	
No.54 Field Ambulance	
No.55 Field Ambulance	
No.56 Field Ambulance	

19th Division

No.57 Field Ambulance	
No.58 Field Ambulance	
No.59 Field Ambulance	

20th Division

No.60 Field Ambulance	
No.61 Field Ambulance	
No.62 Field Ambulance	

21st Division

No.63 Field Ambulance	Territorial Force Field Ambulance 2/2nd West Lancs
No.64 Field Ambulance	Territorial Force Field Ambulance 2/3rd West Lancs
No.65 Field Ambulance	Territorial Force Field Ambulance 3/3rd West Lancs

22nd Division

No.66 Field Ambulance	Moved to Salonika Nov 1915
No.67 Field Ambulance	Moved to Salonika Nov 1915
No.68 Field Ambulance	Moved to Salonika Nov 1915

23rd Division

No.69 Field Ambulance	Moved to Italy Nov 1917
No.70 Field Ambulance	Moved to Italy Nov 1917
No.71 Field Ambulance	Moved to Italy Nov 1917

24th Division

No.72 Field Ambulance	
No.73 Field Ambulance	
No.74 Field Ambulance	

25th Division

No.75 Field Ambulance	
No.76 Field Ambulance	
No.77 Field Ambulance	

26th Division

No.78 Field Ambulance	Moved to Salonika Jan 1916
No.79 Field Ambulance	Moved to Salonika Dec 1915
No.80 Field Ambulance	Moved to Salonika Jan 1916

27th Division

No.81 Field Ambulance	1/1st Home Counties Field Ambulance. Moved to Salonika Nov 1915
No.82 Field Ambulance	1/2nd Home Counties Field Ambulance. Moved to Salonika Nov 1915
No.83 Field Ambulance	1/3rd Home Counties Field Ambulance. Moved to Salonika Nov 1915

28th Division

No.84 Field Ambulance	1/2nd London Field Ambulance. Moved to Alexandria for Salonika Oct 1915
No.85 Field Ambulance	1/3rd London Field Ambulance. Moved to Alexandria for Salonika Oct 1915
No.86 Field Ambulance	1/2nd Northumbrian Field Ambulance. Moved to Alexandria for Salonika Oct 1915

29th Division

No.87 Field Ambulance	1/1st West Lancs Field Ambulance. Previously in Egypt
No.88 Field Ambulance	1/1st East Anglian Field Ambulance. Previously in Egypt
No.89 Field Ambulance	1/1st Highland Field Ambulance. Previously in Egypt

32nd Division

No.90 Field Ambulance	
No.91 Field Ambulance	
No.92 Field Ambulance	

31st Division

No.93 Field Ambulance	Previously in Egypt
No.94 Field Ambulance	Previously in Egypt
No.95 Field Ambulance	Previously in Egypt

30th Division

No.96 Field Ambulance	County Palatine Field Ambulance
No.97 Field Ambulance	County Palatine Field Ambulance
No.98 Field Ambulance	1/2nd West Lancs Field Ambulance

33rd Division

No.99 Field Ambulance	
No.101 Field Ambulance	
No.19 Field Ambulance	
No.100 Field Ambulance	Previously relieving No. 19 Field Ambulance 2 Division

34th Division

No.102 Field Ambulance	
No.103 Field Ambulance	
No.104 Field Ambulance	

35th Division

No.105 Field Ambulance	
No.106 Field Ambulance	
No.107 Field Ambulance	

36th Division

No.108 Field Ambulance	
No.109 Field Ambulance	
No.110 Field Ambulance	

16th Division

No.111 Field Ambulance	
No.112 Field Ambulance	
No.113 Field Ambulance	

38th Division

No.129 Field Ambulance	
No.130 Field Ambulance	
No.131 Field Ambulance	

39th Division

No.132 Field Ambulance	
No.133 Field Ambulance	
No.134 Field Ambulance	

40th Division

No. 135 Field Ambulance	
No. 136 Field Ambulance	
No. 137 Field Ambulance	

41st Division

No.138 Field Ambulance	
No.139 Field Ambulance	
No.140 Field Ambulance	
No.141 Field Ambulance	Joined 1 Division Aug 1915
No.142 Field Ambulance	Joined 3 Division Aug 1915

42nd East Lancs Division

1/1st East Lancs Field Ambulance	Previously in Egypt
1/2nd East Lancs Field Ambulance	Previously in Egypt
1/3rd East Lancs Field Ambulance	Previously in Egypt

46th North Midland Division

1/1st North Midland Field Ambulance	
1/2nd North Midland Field Ambulance	
1/3rd North Midland Field Ambulance	

47th (2nd) London Division

4th London Field Ambulance	
5th London Field Ambulance	
6th London Field Ambulance	

48th South Midland Division

1/1st South Midland Field Ambulance	Moved to Italy Nov 1917
1/2nd South Midland Field Ambulance	Moved to Italy Nov 1917
1/3rd South Midland Field Ambulance	Moved to Italy Nov 1917

49th West Riding Division

1/1st West Riding Field Ambulance	
1/2nd West Riding Field Ambulance	
1/3rd West Riding Field Ambulance	

50th Northumbrian Division

1/1st Northumbrian Field Ambulance	
2/2nd Northumbrian Field Ambulance	
1/3rd Northumbrian Field Ambulance	

51st Highland Division

2/1st Highland Field Ambulance	
1/2nd Highland Field Ambulance	
1/3rd Highland Field Ambulance	

52nd Lowland Division

1/1st Lowland Field Ambulance	Previously in Egypt
1/2nd Lowland Field Ambulance	Previously in Egypt
1/3rd Lowland Field Ambulance	Previously in Egypt

55th West Lancs Division

1/3rd West Lancs Field Ambulance	
2/1st West Lancs Field Ambulance	
2/1st Wessex Field Ambulance	

56th (1st) London Division

2/1st London Field Ambulance	
2/2nd London Field Ambulance	
2/3rd London Field Ambulance	

57th (2nd) West Lancs Division

3/2nd West Lancs Field Ambulance	
2/2nd Wessex Field Ambulance	
2/3rd Wessex Field Ambulance	

58th (2/1st) London Division

2/1st Home Counties Field Ambulance	
2/2nd Home Counties Field Ambulance	
2/3rd Home Counties Field Ambulance	

59th (2nd) North Midland Division

2/1st North Midland Field Ambulance	
2/2nd North Midland Field Ambulance	
2/3rd North Midland Field Ambulance	

60th (2/2nd) London Division

2/4th London Field Ambulance	Moved to Salonika Nov 1916
2/5th London Field Ambulance	Moved to Salonika Nov 1916
2/6th London Field Ambulance	Moved to Salonika Dec 1916

61st (1st) South Midland Division

2/1st South Midland Field Ambulance	
2/2nd South Midland Field Ambulance	
2/3rd South Midland Field Ambulance	

62nd (2nd) West Riding Division

2/1st West Riding Field Ambulance	
2/2nd West Riding Field Ambulance	
2/3rd West Riding Ambulance	

63rd (RN) Division

No. 148 Field Ambulance	Formerly 1st RN Field Ambulance
No. 149 Field Ambulance	Formerly 2nd RN Field Ambulance
No. 150 Field Ambulance	Formerly 3rd RN Field Ambulance

66th (2nd) East Lancs Division

2/1st E Lancs Field Ambulance	Relieved No. 76 Field Ambulance 9 Division Sep 1918

2/2nd E Lancs Field Ambulance
2/3rd E Lancs Field Ambulance

74th Division	
No.229 Field Ambulance	Previously in Egypt
No.230 Field Ambulance	Previously in Egypt
No.231 Field Ambulance	Previously in Egypt

Cavalry	
No.1 Cavalry Field Ambulance	
No.2 Cavalry Field Ambulance	
No.3 Cavalry Field Ambulance	
No.4 Cavalry Field Ambulance	
No.5 Cavalry Field Ambulance	
No.6 Cavalry Field Ambulance	
No.7 Cavalry Field Ambulance	
No.8 Cavalry Field Ambulance	
No.9 Cavalry Field Ambulance	

New Zealand	
No.1 New Zealand Field Ambulance	Previously in Egypt
No.2 New Zealand Field Ambulance	Previously in Egypt
No.3 New Zealand Field Ambulance	Previously in Egypt
No.4 New Zealand Field Ambulance	Attached 4th NZ Infantry Brigade

Australia	
No.1 Australian Field Ambulance	Previously in Egypt
No.2 Australian Field Ambulance	Previously in Egypt
No.3 Australian Field Ambulance	Previously in Egypt
No.4 Australian Field Ambulance	Previously in Egypt
No.5 Australian Field Ambulance	Previously in Egypt
No.6 Australian Field Ambulance	Previously in Egypt
No.7 Australian Field Ambulance	Previously in Egypt
No.8 Australian Field Ambulance	Previously in Egypt
No.9 Australian Field Ambulance	
No.10 Australian Field Ambulance	
No.11 Australian Field Ambulance	
No.12 Australian Field Ambulance	Previously in Egypt
No.13 Australian Field Ambulance	Previously in Egypt
No.14 Australian Field Ambulance	Previously in Egypt
No.15 Australian Field Ambulance	Previously in Egypt

South Africa	
No.1 South African Field Ambulance	Attached 9 Division then 66th Division

Canada

No.1 Canadian Field Ambulance	
No.2 Canadian Field Ambulance	
No.3 Canadian Field Ambulance	
No.4 Canadian Field Ambulance	
No.5 Canadian Field Ambulance	
No.6 Canadian Field Ambulance	
No.7 Canadian Cavalry Field Ambulance	
No.8 Canadian Field Ambulance	
No.9 Canadian Field Ambulance	
No.10 Canadian Field Ambulance	
No.11 Canadian Field Ambulance	
No.12 Canadian Field Ambulance	
No.13 Canadian Field Ambulance	
No.14 Canadian Field Ambulance	

3rd (Lahore) Division	
No.7 British Field Ambulance	Moved to Mesopotamia Dec 1915
No.8 British Field Ambulance	Moved to Mesopotamia Dec 1915
No.111 Indian Field Ambulance	Moved to Mesopotamia Dec 1915
No.112 Indian Field Ambulance	Moved to Mesopotamia Dec 1915
No.113 Indian Field Ambulance	Moved to Mesopotamia Dec 1915

7th (Meerut) Division	
No.19 British Field Ambulance	Moved to Mesopotamia Dec 1915
No.20 British Field Ambulance	Moved to Mesopotamia Dec 1915
No.128 Indian Field Ambulance	Moved to Mesopotamia Dec 1915
No.129 Indian Field Ambulance	Moved to Mesopotamia Dec 1915
No.130 Indian Field Ambulance	Moved to Mesopotamia Dec 1915

1st Indian Cavalry Division	(4th Cavalry Division ex Oct 1916)
Ambala Field Ambulance	Moved to Egypt Mar 1918
Sialkote Field Ambulance	Moved to Egypt Mar 1918
Lucknow Field Ambulance	Moved to Egypt Mar 1918

2nd Indian Cavalry Division	(5th Cavalry Division ex. Oct 1916)
Secunderabad Cavalry Field Ambulance	Moved to Egypt Apr 1918
Meerut Cavalry Field Ambulance (No.119)	Moved to Egypt Apr 1918
Mhow Cavalry Field Ambulance (No.104)	Moved to Egypt Apr 1918
Jodhpur Cavalry Field Ambulance (No.132)	Moved to Egypt Apr 1918

MOTOR AMBULANCE CONVOYS

No.1 Motor Ambulance Convoy	
No.2 Motor Ambulance Convoy	Formed by British Red Cross Society
No.3 Motor Ambulance Convoy	
No.4 Motor Ambulance Convoy	Formed by British Red Cross Society
No.5 Motor Ambulance Convoy	Formed by Captain du Cros
No.6 Motor Ambulance Convoy	Formed by Captain du Cros
No.7 Motor Ambulance Convoy Moved to Salonika 1916	Cars presented by Maharaja of Gwalior.
No.8 Motor Ambulance Convoy Society	Cars presented by Scottish Red Cross
No.9 Motor Ambulance Convoy	Moved to Salonika Jan 1916
No.10 Motor Ambulance Convoy	
No.11 Motor Ambulance Convoy	
No.12 Motor Ambulance Convoy	
No.13 Motor Ambulance Convoy	
No.14 Motor Ambulance Convoy	
No.15 Motor Ambulance Convoy	
No.16 Motor Ambulance Convoy	British Red Cross Society convoy
No. 20 Motor Ambulance Convoy	
No.21 Motor Ambulance Convoy	
N0.22 Motor Ambulance Convoy	
No.24 Motor Ambulance Convoy	
No.25 Motor Ambulance Convoy	
No.26 Motor Ambulance Convoy	Moved to Italy Nov 1917
No.27 Motor Ambulance Convoy	
No.30 Motor Ambulance Convoy	
No.31 Motor Ambulance Convoy	
No.36 Motor Ambulance Convoy	
No.37 Motor Ambulance Convoy	
No.42 Motor Ambulance Convoy	
No.43 Motor Ambulance Convoy	
No.44 Motor Ambulance Convoy	
No.47 Motor Ambulance Convoy	

AMBULANCE FLOTILLAS

No.1 Ambulance Flotilla	Four barges at Rouen provided by British Water Ambulance Fund. Demobilized Nov 1915
No.2 Ambulance Flotilla	
No.3 Ambulance Flotilla	Demobilised Dec 1916 to Mar 1917

No.4 Ambulance Flotilla	Demobilised Nov 1917 to Mar 1918
No.5 Ambulance Flotilla	

AMBULANCE TRAINS

No.1 Ambulance Train	Formed from French rolling stock
No.2 Ambulance Train	Formed from French rolling stock
No.3 Ambulance Train	Formed from French rolling stock
No.4 Ambulance Train	Formed from French rolling stock
No.5 Ambulance Train	Formed from French rolling stock
No.6 Ambulance Train	Formed from French rolling stock
No.7 Ambulance Train	Formed from French rolling stock
No.8 Ambulance Train	Formed from French rolling stock
No.9 Ambulance Train	Formed from French rolling stock
No.10 Ambulance Train	Formed from French rolling stock
No.11 Ambulance Train	Formed from French rolling stock. British Red Cross Society Train
No.12 Ambulance Train	GE & L and NW Railways rolling stock
No.14 Ambulance Train	LB & SC Railway and L & NW Railway, partly the gift of Lord and Lady Michelham
No.15 Ambulance Train	Birmingham Carriage & Wagon Co. Presented by Princess Christian's Fund
No.16 Ambulance Train	Great Western Railway. Presented by UK Flour Millers' Association
No.17 Ambulance Train	Great Eastern Railway, partly the gift of UK Flour Millers' Association
No.18 Ambulance Train	Great Western Railway. Moved to Italy Nov 1917
No.19 Ambulance Train	Great Western Railway
No.20 Ambulance Train	Great Eastern Railway
No.21 Ambulance Train	London & North Western Railway
No.22 Ambulance Train	London & North Western Railway
No.23 Ambulance Train	Caledonian Railway
No.24 Ambulance Train	London & York Railway
No.25 Ambulance Train	London, Brighton & South Coast Railway
No.26 Ambulance Train	Great Western Railway
No.27 Ambulance Train	Great Western Railway
No.28 Ambulance Train	Great Eastern Railway
No.29 Ambulance Train	London & York Railway
No.30 Ambulance Train	London & North Western Railway
No.31 Ambulance Train	London & North Western Railway
No.32 Ambulance Train	London & North Western Railway
No.33 Ambulance Train	Great Western Railway

No.34 Ambulance Train	Midland Railway
No.35 Ambulance Train	London & South Western Railway
No.36 Ambulance Train	Great Eastern Railway
No.37 Ambulance Train	NE Railway
No.38 Ambulance Train	London Railway. In workshop Sep 1917 to Feb 1918. Demobilized Oct 1918
No.39 Ambulance Train	Great Western Railway
No.41 Ambulance Train	London & North Western Railway
No.42 Ambulance Train	London & York Railway
No.43 Ambulance Train	Great Western Railway

APPENDIX B

EXTENDED SCALE OF EQUIPMENT FOR CASUALTY CLEARING STATIONS IN FRANCE

MEMORANDUM ISSUED BY THE QUARTERMASTER-GENERAL AT GENERAL HEADQUARTERS ON 17 SEPTEMBER 1917.

1. In view of the recent heavy demands for the issue to Casualty Clearing Stations of equipment in excess of the authorised scale, it has been found necessary to consider the whole question of the functions which a Casualty Clearing Station is now required to perform, and the scale of equipment necessary for the purpose.

2. The decisions arrived at are as follows:–

(a) That although the functions of a Casualty Clearing Station are still unchanged, i.e.,

(i) To provide hospital accommodation, nursing and treatment for patients unfit for further transport, i.e., the Hospital Section;

(ii) To provide temporary surgical treatment, shelter and food for patients pending transfer to the Base, i.e., the Evacuation Section;

(iii) To retain slighter cases of sickness and wounds pending return to duty or transfer to Rest Stations, i.e., the Convalescent Section; the standard of accommodation and comfort which it is necessary to maintain has increased.

(b) That the scale of equipment should be such as will provide for:–

(i) A Hospital Section – the standard being that of a General Hospital equipped with 200 beds;

(ii) Evacuation and Convalescent Section – the standard of equipment being based on the original Casualty Clearing Station but allowing for 800 patients on stretchers or paillasses;

(c) That each Casualty Clearing Station will be so organised that it will be capable of moving forward at any time as a Casualty Clearing Station with accommodation for 200 wounded on the Old scale, in order to form a nucleus pending the establishment of the bulk of the Casualty Clearing Station gradually on the new site.

3. In accordance with (b) above, the attached Scale of Equipment has been drawn up for future guidance. This represents the maximum amount of equipment considered necessary to equip fully a Casualty Clearing Station, when no accommodation in buildings or huts is available, but it is to be understood that only so much of it as is actually required for the needs of the moment is to be demanded, and that when circumstances change, any equipment which becomes surplus to requirements should be returned to the Base.

4. Equipment already drawn in excess of the above scale for Casualty Clearing Stations engaged in the present operations may be retained until such operations are over, but no demands for replacements of any articles in excess of the new scale can be entertained unless put forward through the DGMS vide paragraph 6 below.

5. In all future indents the scale of each article as now authorised and the number actually in possession must be shown.

6. As it is considered that the new scale will meet all necessary requirements, it has been decided that GRO 1198 shall be cancelled. If exceptional circumstances should render it necessary to provide any special stores in excess of scale, either for Casualty Clearing Stations or Field Ambulances, application should be made to the DGMS, General Headquarters.

7. It is to be understood that the decision in 6 above covers stores for Rest Stations since these should be supplied from the equipment of Field Ambulances (FS Regulations, Part II, Section 89 (5), and that,

consequently, if any stores required cannot be found from the Field Ambulances, the application must be sent to DGMS. An exception may be made in the case of tents, and, in cases in which the bell tents issued to Field Ambulances are not considered suitable for Main Dressing Stations, Marquees SS up to a maximum of 48 per Corps may be demanded without further authority.

8. A General Routine Order on the subject is about to be published, but in the meantime, I shall be glad if you will issue instructions on the lines given.

MODIFIED SCALE OF EQUIPMENT FOR CASUALTY CLEARING STATIONS

	800 Patients Enlarged CCS	200 Patients General Hospital	Total CCS
Axes, hand, Mk II	4	-	4
Boxes, lantern, distinguishing, double	-	-	2
Boxes, stationary, field	-	12	12
Buckets, water, GS, canvas	24	-	24
Flags, distinguishing, HP	-	-	2
Flags, distinguishing, crossbars	-	-	2
Flags, distinguishing, poles	-	-	2
Forms, dining tent	68	32	100
Hooks, bill	5	5	10
Hooks, reaping, small	8	-	8
Kettles, camp, oval, 12-quarts	24	-	24
Lanterns, distinguishing, white	-	-	4
Lanterns, tent, folding	-	-	2
Sheets, ground	800	-	800
Stools, camp	16	32	48
Stoves, Soyers	8	4	12
Tables, camp	8	8	16
Tables, portable, F.S.	40	26	66
Tents, complete – marquee H.P.S.	60	20	80
Tents, C.S.L., for use of staff	-	-	35
Tents, C.D.L., for use of staff	-	-	15
Tents, store	-	-	1
Tents, marquee, small double	-	-	1
Axes, pick	16	5	21

	800 Patients Enlarged CCS	200 Patients General Hospital	Total CCS
Shovels, G.S.	16	9	25
Baskets, bottle, hand	16	-	16
Boards, bedhead	-	212	212
Boards, knife	-	-	6
Boxes, salt, 7 lbs.	2	-	2
Bottles, water, table, 1-quart	-	8	8
Bottles, water, toilet	-	2	2
Brooms, bass	16	8	24
Brushes, bedpan	-	20	20
Brushes, feeders	30	30	60
Brushes, scrubbing, hand	8	20	28
Brushes, stencil	2	1	3
Brushes, sweeping, long	-	20	20
Brushes, washing	24	-	24
Brushes, whitewash, hair, 6 oz.	12	-	12
Chairs, arm, H.P. folding	-	32	32
Chairs, officers, folding F.A.	-	32	32
Clothes horses	-	1	1
Cups, tea, earthen	-	9	9
Feeders, earthen	-	40	40
Glasses, looking	-	12	12
Inhalers	4	-	4
Lamps F.S.	160	40	200
Lamps, glasses (spare)	16	4	20
Lamps, operating F.A.	8	1	9
Lamps, hand, acetylene	40	-	40
Lamps, operating, acetylene, large	12	-	12
Measures, glass, 4 oz.	-	20	20
Measures, glass, 2 oz.	-	40	40
Mops, common	-	2	2
Pins, rolling	-	1	1
Refrigerators	-	1	1
Safes, bread	-	1	1
Safes, meat	-	1	1
Saucers, tea, earthen	-	9	9
Screens, bedside	-	8	8
Sponges, bath	32	4	36
Squeezers, lemon	8	1	9

	800 Patients Enlarged CCS	200 Patients General Hospital	Total CCS
Strainers, hair, 15 ins.	-	1	1
Tables, bedside	-	208	208
Trays, bed	-	28	28
Trays, dinner	-	16	16
Tumblers, half-pint	-	40	40
Tumblers, toilet	-	2	2
Tumblers, wine	-	10	10
Urinals, glass (or earthen)	-	20	20
Washhand stands H.P.	-	1	1
Portable clarifier and steriliser	1	-	1
Slates, plain	-	1	1
Balances, spring, 200 lbs.	1	-	1
Balances, spring, 30 lbs.	2	-	2
Basins, enamelled, 14 ins.	80	40	120
Basins, enamelled, 7.25 ins.	80	58	138
Basins, enamelled, 6 ins.	800	212	1,012
Basins, washing, zinc, 11 ins.	160	-	160
Baths, arm	8	4	12
Baths, foot	-	10	10
Baths, long, open	-	2	2
Bells, hand, press	-	1	1
Boilers, tea or coffee	-	2	2
Boilers, water, tin	8	4	12
Bowls, shaving	-	4	4
Boxes, dressing	16	8	24
Cans, 3 galls	8	20	28
Cans, oil, feeding, half-pint	4	-	4
Cans, oil, 5.5 pints	4	-	4
Cans, oil, 9 pints	2	-	2
Carts, hand, slop	-	2	2
Castors, pepper, enamelled	-	20	20
Clippers, hair	4	8	12
Colanders, tin 10.5 ins	-	2	2
Corkscrews	20	-	20
Covers, tin, 6.25 ins	100	-	100
Cradles, fracture	-	8	8
Cups, egg, enamelled	-	60	60
Cups, canteen, drinking, 1 pint	200	-	200
Cups, spitting, enamelled	60	40	100

	800 Patients Enlarged CCS	200 Patients General Hospital	Total CCS
Dishes, meat, tin, 17.5 ins.	-	2	2
Dredgers, flour	-	1	1
Forks, carving	-	2	2
Forks, flesh	4	-	4
Forks, table, large	-	16	16
Forks, toasting	-	2	2
Feeders, enamelled	120	-	120
Funnels, tin, half-pint	1	1	2
Graters, bread	-	1	1
Gridirons, fluted	-	1	1
Implements, butcher's, cases, wood, filled	2	1	3
Jugs, enamelled, F.A., 2 quart	16	1	17
Jugs, enamelled, F.A., 1 quart	-	1	1
Kettles, tea, 2 quart	-	20	20
Kettles, cooking	32	-	32
Knives, bread	-	1	1
Knives, carving	-	2	2
Knives, opening, tins	20	-	20
Knives, table, large	-	16	16
Ladles, cooks F.A.	8	2	10
Ladles, soup	-	1	1
Machines, mincing, large	4	-	4
Measures, milk	-	1	1
Measures, tin, half-gall.	-	1	1
Measures, tin, one quart	-	1	1
Measures, tin, 1 pint	-	1	1
Measures, tin, half-pint	-	1	1
Measures, wine & spirit, one quart	-	1	1
Measures, wine & spirit, one pint	-	1	1
Measures, wine & spirit, half-pint	-	1	1
Measures, wine & spirit, one gill	-	1	1
Measures, wine & spirit, half-gill	-	1	1
Pails, slop	-	20	20
Pails I.G.	32	20	52

	800 Patients Enlarged CCS	200 Patients General Hospital	Total CCS
Panniers G.S.	64	-	64
Pannikins, 1 pint	-	200	200
Pans, bed, enamelled	32	20	52
Pans, frying, 9 ins, enamelled	-	8	8
Picks, ice	2	-	2
Plates, dinner, enamelled	800	229	1,029
Pots, chamber, enamelled	-	32	32
Pots, mustard, enamelled	-	16	16
Pots, tea, enamelled	4	12	16
Salt cellars, iron	-	32	32
Saucepans, F.A., nests	4	-	4
Saws, butcher's, bow, 20 ins.	-	1	1
Scissors, haircutting	16	16	32
Scissors, lamp	2	-	2
Scissors, nail	10	-	10
Scoops, hand, flour	4	-	4
Shapes, pudding	24	40	64
Skewers	6	-	6
Skewers (12 to a set), sets	4	-	4
Spittoons	-	16	16
Spoons, e.p., dessert	-	16	16
Spoons, e.p., egg	-	3	3
Spoons, e.p., tea	-	8	8
Spoons, gravy	-	2	2
Spoons, n.s., mustard, large	-	16	16
Spoons, n.s., salt, large	-	32	32
Spoons, n.s., tea	-	16	16
Stands, cruet, large	-	1	1
Stools, close, F.A., nests of 8	4	9	13
Stoves, Primus	20	4	24
Stoves, portable	4	4	8
Strainers, gravy, round	-	1	1
Trays, diet	-	16	16
Trays, soap, enamelled	-	26	26
Tubs, ablution	-	4	4
Tubs, washing, 8 gall., iron	-	6	6
Urinals, zinc	128	-	128
Warmers, food, spirit lamp	-	5	5
Whisks, egg	-	1	1

	800 Patients Enlarged CCS	200 Patients General Hospital	Total CCS
Disinfectors, Thresh	1	-	1
Blankets G.S.	1,600	600	2,200
Bolsters, hospital	-	224	224
Cases, bolster, barrack coir	800	12	812
Cases, paillasse	800	12	812
Cases, slip, bolster, hospital	-	260	260
Cases, slip, mattress	-	312	312
Cases, slip, pillow, large	-	617	617
Cases, slip, pillow, small	-	40	40
Counterpanes, hospital	-	232	232
Mattresses, hospital	-	224	224
Pillows, hospital, feather	200	208	408
Pillows, hospital, hair, large	-	224	224
Pillows, hospital, hair, small	-	12	12
Sheets	1,920	1,200	3,120
Bedsteads, folding Mk II	-	208	208
Mattresses, spring	-	208	208
Cloths, bedpan covering	-	40	40
Cloths, distinctive	-	80	80
Cloths, medicine	-	80	80
Cloths, table	-	80	80
Cloths, tea	400	480	880
Dusters	-	80	80
Flags, Union	-	-	2
Napkins, ophthalmia	-	40	40
Napkins, table	-	24	24
Flannel, white, yards	48	-	48
Nets, potato	-	10	10
Netting, mosquito, yards	-	30	30
Stretchers, ambulance	840	8	848
Tapes, chest-measuring	8	-	8
Tow, carbolized, pounds	240	-	240
Towels, bath	-	12	12
Towels, hand, hospital	1,600	800	2,400
Towels, operating	320	16	336
Towels, round	-	120	120
Towels, Turkish	-	300	300
Wringers, fomentation	-	16	16
Straps, securing, 1 ins. x 84 ins.	28	-	28

	800 Patients Enlarged CCS	200 Patients General Hospital	Total CCS
Carriages, ambulance, stretcher	16	4	20
Bicycles	4	-	4
Waistcoats, cardigan	200	40	240
Trousers, duck, universal, pairs	-	6	6
Aprons, cook's, dowlas	18	6	24
Aprons, operating	40	16	56
Frocks, dowlas	-	6	6
Coats, great, drab, mixture, D.M.	100	40	140
Slippers, leather, pairs	50	228	278
Gowns, serge, lined	-	249	249
Handkerchiefs	800	624	1,424
Jackets, sleeping	400	40	440
Neckerchiefs	-	312	312
Trousers, serge, lined	-	312	312
Trousers, pyjama, sleeping	1,200	40	1,240
Waistcoats, serge, lined	-	240	240
Buttons, bone, white, large, gross	12	2	14
Buttons, zinc, large, gross	12	2	14
Buttons, zinc, small, gross	12	2	14
Needles, darning	100	-	100
Needles, sewing, assorted	100	-	100
Cotton, white, mercerized, No.18, reels	50	-	50
Worsted, blue-grey, pounds	4	-	4
Bags, tool, shoemaker's, filled	-	-	2
Brushes, shaving	8	16	24
Combs, hair	64	16	80
Drawers, flannel	-	312	312
Dressings, field	98	-	98
Forks	800	208	1,008
Knives, table	800	208	1,008
Razors	8	-	8
Shirts, cotton, made	-	561	561
Shirts, cotton, for helpless patients	-	62	62

	800 Patients Enlarged CCS	200 Patients General Hospital	Total CCS
Shirts, flannel, white, ordinary, made	900	312	1,212
Shirts, flannel, white, for helpless patients	300	104	404
Socks, worsted	1,600	624	2,224
Spoons	800	212	1,012
Strops, razor	8	-	8
Aprons, operating, waterproof	144	-	144

APPENDIX C

THE BOMBING OF THE CANADIAN HOSPITAL AT DOULLENS 29/30 MAY 1918

EXCERPT FROM THE WAR DIARY OF NO.3 CANADIAN STATIONARY HOSPITAL.

On the night of 29–30 of May hostile aeroplanes were heard in the area. The night was clear and the moon shining. About 12.25 am hostile aeroplane passed over the hospital, dropped a flare, and immediately a bomb was dropped which struck the main building over the sergeants' quarters, Ward S.6 (officers' ward), operating theatre and x-ray room which collapsed immediately. Almost instantly a fire broke out and the whole group of buildings in the upper area were threatened. The alarm was given at once and every effort made to save the patients and combat the fire. The Nursing Sisters and orderlies worked splendidly and with the assistance of other members of the unit rapidly removed all patients to places of safety. There were no other casualties other than those killed by the bombs. During the work of rescue and while other members of the unit were combating the fire, the aeroplane returned and dropped more bombs, fortunately without doing any damage. At this time the flames were mounting sky high and the whole upper area was clearly illuminated and the buildings sharply delineated. The Red Crosses on the buildings being very visible so there was no excuse for his not knowing that it was a hospital. The sergeants were in their quarters and the entire number were casualties. Ward S.6 (the officers' ward) was fortunately only partially filled with patients but unfortunately all those in their ward were killed by the bomb, including the Nursing Sister who was on duty. Immediately below this were the x-ray room and the operating theatre.

Three surgical teams were on duty that night but two had completed their operation and had gone for their midnight meal. The other team (Capt. E. E. Meek C.A.M.C. and Lieut. A. F. H. Sage M.O.R.C. U.S.A. were finishing their operation and they, their patient, Sisters A. McPherson and E. L. Pringle, the orderlies and stretcher bearers, were all victims of the bomb. During the work of rescue and in the endeavour to save the buildings from fire, we received splendid assistance from three companies of French soldiers and from the English soldiers quartered in Doullens. With their timely aid we were able to save the west wing of the main buildings. The night was clear and bright. There should have been no difficulty in the airmen recognizing it as a hospital. The plane is stated to have been at a height of about 6,000 feet. The hospital is well marked with Red Crosses which airmen say are quite visible from the air. There is no doubt that the occupants of the aeroplane knew it was a hospital for when they came back and dropped bombs a second time, the flames clearly illuminated the Red Crosses on the buildings. The hospital, being in the citadel, is surrounded on three sides by fields and on the fourth by a French hospital. There were no camps of troops or dumps of any description in the vicinity of the hospital. 18 Nursing Sisters proceeded to No.2 Canadian General Hospital for duty. N/Ss F.D. McLaughlin and H.A. McLaughlin struck off strength on proceeding to No.8 Canadian General Hospital for duty. Casualties: personnel killed 2 officers, 3 Nursing Sisters, 9 other ranks and 7 other ranks attached. Wounded 1 Nursing Sister, 10 other ranks and 3 other ranks attached. Patients killed officers 7, other ranks 4. Admissions nil. Discharges nil. The funeral of the victims of the air raid took place this afternoon and a very impressive service was held. Bishop Fallon of London, Ontario who came to visit the hospital on the 30th, very kindly took part in the service.

Signed by: *Lieutenant Colonel*
Clifford H. Reason DSO, CAMC
Officer Commanding
No. 3 Canadian Stationary Hospital

APPENDIX D

SOME MEDICAL STATISTICS FOR THE WESTERN FRONT 1914–1918

BASED ON FIGURES EXTRACTED FROM THE OFFICIAL HISTORY.

CASUALTIES

British and Dominion Casualties (approx.) in France and Flanders 1914-1918

	1914	1915	1916	1917	1918	Total
Killed in Action	13,009	48,604	107,411	131,761	80,476	381,261
Died of Wounds	3,657	14,904	36,879	49,832,	46,084	151,356
Died of disease or injury	508	2,907	5,841	8,422	13,785	31,463
Total Deaths	**17,174**	**66,415**	**150,131**	**190,015**	**140,345**	**564,080**
Missing & taken Prisoner of War	26,511	24,556	43,675	53,794	171,288	319,824
Wounded	55,689	224,963	463,697	514,862	578,402	1,837,613
Sick or Injured	78,049	576,831	638,080	1,033,844	1,169,584	3,496,388
Total Casualties	**177,423**	**892,765**	**1,295,583**	**1,792,515**	**2,059,619**	**6,217,905**

STRENGTHS

	1914	1915	1916	1917	1918
British & Dominion Troops	190,000	616,086	1,322,075	1,894,511	1,857,026
Indian, African & Others	24,572	35,568	12,299	11,462	14,500
Camp Followers & Labour Corps	6,000	10,688	2,681	62,905	117,845
Total Strengths	220,572	662,342	1,337,055	1,968,878	1,989,371

HOSPITAL ADMISSIONS & DISPOSALS

	Wounded	Sick & Injured
Admissions	1,981,850	3,462,531
Returned to Duty	584,959	2,396,273
Evacuated Overseas	1,245,535	1,034,160
Deaths	151,356	32,098

Deaths as a percentage of admissions to Medical Units in France & Flanders: Wounded 7.64% Sick and Injured 1.62%

CASUALTIES SUFFERED BY DIFFERENT ARMS

Analysed from casualties in five major Western Front battles: Somme 1916, Arras, Messines, Ypres and Cambrai 1917.

Infantry	88.18%
Royal Artillery	6.06%
Machine Gun Corps	1.75%
Royal Engineers	1.55%
Royal Army Medical Corps	.83%
Cavalry	.29%
Royal Flying Corps	.27%
Tank Corps	.25%
Army Service Corps	.13%
Miscellaneous Units	.66%
Headquarters Staff	.03%
100%	

CASUALTIES EVACUATED TO UK 1914–1918

France and Flanders	2,260,880	91.89%
All other theatres	199,122	8.11%
Total from all theatres	**2,460,002**	**100%**

WOUNDS INFLICTED BY DIFFERENT WEAPONS

Analysed from 212,659 casualties admitted to Casualty Clearing Stations.

	Number	Percentage
Shells, Trench Mortars, etc.	124,425	58.51%
Rifle or Machine Gun Bullets	82,901	38.98%
Bombs and Grenades	4,649	2.19%
Bayonets	684	.32%
	212,659	**100%**

REGIONAL INCIDENCE OF WOUNDS INFLICTED BY DIFFERENT WEAPONS

Analysed from 48,290 casualties admitted to Casualty Clearing Stations.

	Bullets (Rifle and Machine Gun)	Shells, Trench Mortars, etc.	Bombs and Grenades
Head, Face and Neck	15%	16.43%	15.03%
Eyes	1.13%	1.61%	2.09%
Shoulder and Back	10.04%	10.71%	8.50%
Chest, front and sides	5.52%	4.26%	3.47%
Abdomen, front and sides	3.94%	3.04%	2.35%
Buttocks	3.91%	3.87%	4.09%
Thighs	11.35%	10.07%	9.11%
Legs	15.16%	15.23%	17.76%
Feet	4.55%	4.03%	4.56%
Arms	12.43%	10.83%	12.05%
Forearms and Elbows	5.13%	3.77%	3.03%
Hands	6.89%	5.79%	6.36%
Multiple	4.95%	10.36%	11.60%
	100%	**100%**	**100%**

TRANSPORT OF THE SICK AND WOUNDED

France and Flanders 1914-1918
§ signifies that no figures are available

	1914	1915	1916	1917	1918	Total
Evacuation from Front to Base						
by Ambulance Train	85,327	383,810	744,616	1,038,993	1,190,761	3,443,507
by Ambulance Barge	0	4,156	18,042	10,112	21,451	53,761
by Motor Ambulance	§	§	§	30,196	22,645	52,841
Total Front to Base	85,327	387,966	762,658	1,079,301	1,234,857	3,550,109
Evacuation from Base to Base						
by Ambulance Train	7,544	87,642	253,907	493,280	768,299	1,610,672
Total Movements	92,871	475,608	1,016,565	1,572,581	2,003,156	5,160,781

DENTAL WORK

Analysis of a 6-month period in 1918.

Treatments	
Fillings	40,692
Extractions	79,434
Sundries	47,139
	167,265
Dentures	
New dentures made	10,966
Dentures repaired	8,293
Dentures sent down for repair	6,421
	25,680
Evacuation	
Cases evacuated to Army Dental Centres	3,004
Cases evacuated to Base Dental Centres	214
	3,218

NON-BATTLE CASUALTIES

Admissions for diseases and other causes, France and Flanders 1914–1918
§ signifies that no figures are available

	1914	1915	1916	1917	1918	Total
Cerebro-Spinal Fever						
Admissions	2	357	393	692	176	1,620
Deaths	1	169	138	192	69	569
Chicken Pox						
Admissions	4	43	83	139	124	393
Deaths	0	0	0	0	0	0
Diphtheria						
Admissions	37	439	1,175	2,273	1,657	5,581
Deaths	6	7	8	20	24	65
Measles						
Admissions	103	1,929	1,912	2,165	1,221	7,330
Deaths	1	12	5	14	4	36
Mumps						
Admissions	22	399	4,333	8,203	2,410	15,367
Deaths	0	0	0	0	0	0
Rubella						
Admissions	1	1,613	5,490	9,418	1,698	18,220
Deaths	0	1	1	9	5	16
Scarlet Fever						
Admissions	79	808	749	563	496	2,695
Deaths	0	14	7	2	4	27
Smallpox						
Admissions	0	1	4	1	6	12
Deaths	0	0	0	0	3	3
Pulmonary Tuberculosis						
Admissions	325	1,541	1,203	1,512	§	4,581
Deaths	10	60	§	§	§	70
Other Tuberculosis						
Admissions	26	359	140	148	§	673
Deaths	2	25	§	§	§	27
Pneumonia						
Admissions	378	1,925	1,497	2,157	1,921	7,878
Deaths	53	241	135	193	352	974
Malaria						
Admissions	1,147	4,297	58	781	2,739	9,022
Deaths	4	4	§	2	4	14

Dysentery

Admissions	861	1,559	5,776	6,025	12,211	26,432
Deaths	4	24	40	46	41	155

Enteric Fever

Admissions	466	3,462	2,738	1,275	376	8,317
Deaths	57	153	30	24	22	286

Influenza

Admissions	1,478	44,392	§	§	313,938	359,808
Deaths	2	23	§	§	§	25

Nephritis

Admissions	104	4,010	9,813	15,214	6,422	35,563
Deaths	4	97	92	201	§	394

Jaundice

Admissions	94	1,492	181	940	1,268	3,975
Deaths	0	14	2	9	6	31

Frost Bite

Admissions	6,447	16,256	§	§	§	22,703
Deaths	12	19	§	§	§	31

Trench Foot

Admissions	§	6,462	§	§	§	6,462
Deaths	§	6	§	§	§	6

Venereal Diseases

Gonorrhoea	2,272	12,378	16,209	30,683	§	61,542
Syphilis	599	3,849	3,583	8,983	§	17,014
Other VDs	420	1,298	4,316	8,842	§	14,876
Total VDs	3,291	17,525	24,108	48,508	§	93,432

SOURCES

The following sources were consulted during preparation of this book.

UNPUBLISHED AND INTERNET SOURCES:

War Diaries of 29th Casualty Clearing Station RAMC 1917–1919, National Archives, Ref: WO95/415.

Correspondence and Papers of Lt Col J.C.G. Carmichael, OBE, MB, Ch.B (Edin), DPH (Cantab), RAMC, private collection.

War Diary of No.3 Canadian Stationary Hospital, 1918.

War Diary of No.1 Canadian Casualty Clearing Station, 1918/19,

Library and Archives Canada: War Diaries of the First World War, www.collectionscanada.gc.ca

War Diaries of Matron-in-Chief BEF France and Flanders, National Archives Ref: WO95/3988, 3989, 3990, 3991. Edited transcription online at www.scarletfinders.co.uk

Northwestern University, Chicago, formation of No.12 Base Hospital, France, www.northwestern.edu/about/historic-moments/turbulent-times/northwestern-university-base-hospital.html

PUBLISHED SOURCES:

Army Diary 1974, Beneath the White Cross: A Short History of Army Nursing Services, (Method Publishing, Golspie, 1974)

Army Diary 1975, Lord Wargraves: A Brief Account of the Work of Sir Fabian Ware, (Method Publishing, Golspie, 1975)

Aston, Sir George, *The Biography of the late Marshal Foch* (Hutchinson, London).

Bean C.E.W., *Official History of Australia in the War of 1914–18, Vol. VI The AIF in France 1918* (Angus & Robertson, Sydney, 1942)

Blake, Robert (ed.), *Private Papers of Douglas Haig 1914–18* (Eyre & Spottiswoode, London, 1952)

Boraston J. (ed.) *Sir Douglas Haig's Despatches* (Dent, London 1979)

Cantile, Lt Gen. Sir Neil, *A History of the Army Medical Department, Vols I and II*, (Churchill Livingstone, Edinburgh, 1974)

Churchill, Winston S., *The World Crisis 1911–1918, Vols. I and II*, (Butterworth, London 1927) & *The Aftermath: A Sequel to The World Crisis* (Butterworth, London, 1929)

Edmonds, Brig. Gen. Sir James, *History of the Great War based on Official Documents: Military Operations France and Belgium 1918, Vols. I–V* (Macmillan, London, 1935–39)

Haber, L.F., *The Poisonous Cloud: Chemical Warfare in the First World War* (Oxford University Press, 1986)

Harbord, James G., *The American Army in France 1917–1919* (Little Brown, Boston 1936)

Hutchinson, John, *Champions of Charity: War and the Rise of the Red Cross* (Westview Press, USA, 1996)

Lloyd George, David, *War Memoirs, Vols I and II* (Odhams, London, 1938)

Longworth, Philip, *The Unending Vigil: A History of the Commonwealth War Graves Commission 1917–1967* (Constable, 1967)

MacPhail, Sir Andrew, *Official Canadian History of the Great War 1914–1919: The Medical Services* (Acland, Ottawa, 1925)

MacPherson, Maj. Gen. Sir W.G., *History of the Great War based on Official Documents: Medical Services Vol. II* (Macmillan, London 1923) and Vol. III (HMSO, 1924)

Miller, H.W., *The Paris Gun* (Harrap, London, 1930)

Mitchell, Maj. T.J. and Smith, Miss G.M., *History of the Great War based on Official Documents: Casualties and Medical Statistics* (HMSO, 1920)

Munby, Lt Col J.E., (ed.) *A History of the 38th (Welsh) Division* (Rees, London 1920)

Smith, Col Fred, *A Short History of the Royal Army Medical Corps* (Gale & Polden, Aldershot, 1929)

INDEX

The abbreviations for regiments shown in this book are intended for ease of recognition and are not, necessarily, the official Army abbreviations.

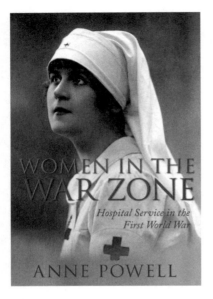

Women in the War Zone: Hospital Service in the First World War by Anne Powell

ISBN 978-0-7509- 5059-6

'An unforgettable book.' *Pennant*

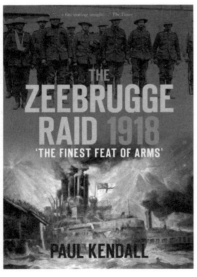

The Zeebrugge Raid: 'The Finest Feat of Arms' by Paul Kendall

ISBN 978-0-7524-5332-3

'Make a point of reading this magnificent book ... one that would grace any library.' *Britain at War*

'A fascinating insight.' *The Times*